Using Gatsby and Netlify CMS

Build Blazing Fast JAMstack Apps Using Gatsby and Netlify CMS

Joe Attardi

Apress®

Using Gatsby and Netlify CMS: Build Blazing Fast JAMstack Apps Using Gatsby and Netlify CMS

Joe Attardi
Billerica, MA, USA

ISBN-13 (pbk): 978-1-4842-6296-2   ISBN-13 (electronic): 978-1-4842-6297-9
https://doi.org/10.1007/978-1-4842-6297-9

Managing Director, Apress Media LLC: Welmoed Spahr
Acquisitions Editor: Louise Corrigan
Development Editor: James Markham
Coordinating Editor: Nancy Chen

Cover designed by eStudioCalamar

Cover image designed by Freepik (www.freepik.com)

Distributed to the book trade worldwide by Springer Science+Business Media New York, 1 New York Plaza, New York, NY 10004. Phone 1-800-SPRINGER, fax (201) 348-4505, e-mail orders-ny@springer-sbm.com, or visit www.springeronline.com. Apress Media, LLC is a California LLC and the sole member (owner) is Springer Science + Business Media Finance Inc (SSBM Finance Inc). SSBM Finance Inc is a Delaware corporation.

For information on translations, please e-mail booktranslations@springernature.com; for reprint, paperback, or audio rights, please e-mail bookpermissions@springernature.com.

Apress titles may be purchased in bulk for academic, corporate, or promotional use. eBook versions and licenses are also available for most titles. For more information, reference our Print and eBook Bulk Sales web page at http://www.apress.com/bulk-sales.

Any source code or other supplementary material referenced by the author in this book is available to readers on GitHub via the book's product page, located at www.apress.com/9781484262962. For more detailed information, please visit http://www.apress.com/source-code.

Printed on acid-free paper

To Liz and Benjamin – you are my whole world.

Table of Contents

About the Author xi

About the Technical Reviewer xiii

Acknowledgments xv

Introduction xvii

Chapter 1: Introduction to Netlify CMS 1

The JAMstack 1

About Netlify 2

What is a CMS? 3

Traditional CMS 3

Headless CMS 4

Netlify CMS 5

    Backends 6

    How it works 7

    Local development 9

    Widgets 9

    Previews 11

Summary 12

Chapter 2: Gatsby Crash Course 13

What is Gatsby? 13

Creating pages 13

GraphQL and Gatsby 14

    The GraphiQL tool 15

Query types 16

    Page queries 16

    Static queries 17

Plugins 19

    Source plugins 19

    Transformer plugins 20

    Other plugins 22

Dynamic page creation 22

Markdown primer 23

    Basic formatting 24

    Front matter 24

Gatsby starters 25

The build process 25

    Data model and GraphQL schema creation 26

    Page creation 26

    Query extraction 26

    Query execution 26

    Static HTML generation 26

Summary 27

Chapter 3: Setting Up the Example Project 29

Prerequisites 29

    Install Git 29

    Install Node.js 29

    Install the Gatsby command line interface 30

    Sign up for GitHub 30

Create a new repository with the starter code 30

Clone the repository 31

Install dependencies and test it out 32

Deploy on Netlify 33

    Sign up 33

    Create a new site 35

A tour of the example project 41

    Directory structure 41

    The Layout component 42

CSS modules 42

Special Gatsby files 43

Summary 44

Chapter 4: Setting Up Netlify CMS **45**

Install dependencies 45

Configuration 45

YAML primer 46

Creating the initial configuration 47

Collections 48

Folder collections 48

Filtered folder collections 48

File collections 48

Configuring the blog collection 49

More about fields 50

Add the Gatsby plugin 50

Commit and deploy 51

Configure Netlify Identity and Git Gateway 51

More about Netlify Identity 54

Summary 55

Chapter 5: The Netlify CMS Application **57**

Registering and logging in 57

Creating a new blog post 59

Publishing the post 62

How publishing works 64

Adding media 65

Alternative media storage options 66

Adding media to a blog post 67

Inserting the image 67

Publishing the updated blog post 69

Summary 70

Chapter 6: Sourcing Blog Data 71

Gatsby plugin configuration 71

Making Gatsby aware of the Markdown files.. 71

Parsing the Markdown data... 73

Querying and displaying the data 74

    Creating a blog post component 75

    Creating a blog list component and querying for data 76

    Using the BlogList component... 77

Adding a second blog post.. 79

Fixing the sort order.. 81

Summary.. 83

Chapter 7: Dynamic Page Creation 85

Gatsby Node APIs... 85

    onCreateNode.. 85

    createPages.. 86

Adding the slug to the blog post data 86

Dynamically creating the blog post pages 87

    Creating the blog post template 88

    Creating the pages 90

Linking to the dynamically generated pages 92

    The Gatsby Link component.. 94

One last tweak 96

Summary.. 98

Chapter 8: Blog Pagination 99

How pagination works 99

Creating some new blog entries 100

Dynamically creating the blog list pages 100

Creating the blog list template page 103

Adding a link to the new blog list page... 108

Updating the index page 110

Summary 112

Chapter 9: Adding More Content **113**

The contentKey field 114

Creating a pages collection 121

Adding the index page data 123

Adding another filesystem source 125

Using the CMS content in the index page 126

Summary 129

Chapter 10: Creating the Coffee Menu **131**

Nested lists 131

Defining the menu page 131

Adding menu items 134

Building the menu page 139

Ease of maintenance 146

Summary 147

Chapter 11: Working with Images **149**

Plugins 149

Adding the plugins to the Gatsby configuration 150

How gatsby-transformer-sharp works 154

GraphQL fragments 155

Using the BackgroundImage component 157

Disabling the "blur-up" effect 159

Fixing the header background 160

Moving the image 160

Modifying the Layout component to use a static query 160

The gatsby-image package 163

Summary 163

Chapter 12: Customizing the CMS **165**

Customizing Netlify CMS 166

Updating the plugin configuration 166

Adding a custom menu preview 168

Refactoring the menu page 168

Creating the preview component 169

Opening the local CMS instance 171

Refactoring the menu page again 172

Updating the preview component 175

Previewing the menu data 176

Summary 179

Chapter 13: The Editorial Workflow **181**

Enabling the editorial workflow 181

Adding some new content 184

Viewing the pull request 185

Viewing the preview 187

Updating the status 188

Finishing up 190

Summary 192

Chapter 14: Wrap Up **193**

Further learning 193

Integration with other frameworks 194

Netlify Identity OAuth 194

Beta features 194

Netlify CMS resources 195

Index **197**

About the Author

 **Joe Attardi** is a software engineer specializing in front-end development. He has over 15 years' experience working with JavaScript, HTML, and CSS and has worked extensively with front-end technologies such as Angular and React. He currently works at Salesforce and has worked in the past with companies such as Dell and Nortel. He is also the author of *Modern CSS*, an Apress title. He lives in the Boston area with his wife and son. You can find him on Twitter at @JoeAttardi.

About the Technical Reviewer

Alexander Nnakwue has a background in Mechanical Engineering from the University of Ibadan, Nigeria, and has been a front-end developer for over 3 years working on both web and mobile technologies. He also has experience as a technical author, writer, and reviewer. He enjoys programming for the Web, and occasionally, you can also find him playing soccer. He was born in Benin City and is currently based in Lagos, Nigeria.

Acknowledgments

I'd like to start by thanking my wonderful wife, Liz, for her constant love and encouragement throughout the whole writing process – and for understanding when I locked myself away in solitude to write. And my little toddler, Benjamin, for giving me much needed breaks from writing for play time.

Thanks to all my friends and family for always supporting and encouraging my interest in computers and technology.

This book began its life as a self-published work, and I'd like to thank Apress for making it what it is today. I'd also like to thank the awesome team at Apress – Louise Corrigan, Nancy Chen, and Jim Markham – for guiding me through the process every step of the way. I appreciate their patience with me as a first-time author.

Thanks to Alexander Nnakwue, the technical reviewer for this book, for his time and excellent feedback, helping make this book even better.

Introduction

In this book, you will learn all about creating a website using Gatsby, getting its content from Netlify CMS, a free content management system from Netlify. We'll start with a bare-bones template project and install and configure Netlify CMS from scratch.

In Chapter 1, we'll look at the JAMstack and what a content management system is. We'll talk about headless CMSs and introduce Netlify CMS.

Chapter 2 is a Gatsby crash course. If you have built a site with Gatsby before, you can probably skip this chapter, as it is a very basic overview of Gatsby. Conversely, if you haven't been exposed to Gatsby before, this introduction should be enough to get you going.

We'll start setting up the example project, a coffee shop website, in Chapter 3. We'll take care of signing up for GitHub and Netlify if you haven't already and also get your version of the example project deployed on Netlify.

In Chapter 4, we'll start adding Netlify CMS to the project. This covers installation of the CMS and creation of the configuration file. We'll set up the blog content and integrate with the Netlify identity service.

In Chapter 5, we'll take a tour of the CMS user interface, and create our first piece of content: a blog post. We'll also look at how to add images to blog posts.

We'll take the content created by the CMS and start integrating that with Gatsby in Chapter 6. We'll configure some Gatsby plugins which will add the blog content to Gatsby's data model.

Chapter 7 is all about creating pages from data. It will introduce the Gatsby Node APIs and show how Gatsby dynamically creates pages by combining data with a page template.

Eventually, we'll end up with too much blog data to show on a single page, so in Chapter 8, we'll learn how to paginate the blog posts. We'll split the blog post listing into several pages (which are also dynamically created).

Up to now, the content on the landing page, such as the hero image and tagline, is managed in the source code. Chapter 9 will explore how to make this content dynamic and editable from Netlify CMS. We'll make several elements of the landing page configurable from the CMS, allowing the page content to be updated without writing a line of code.

In Chapter 10, we'll create a menu for the coffee shop. We'll create new content definitions in the CMS configuration for menu categories, items, and prices.

Gatsby has some plugins that can help generate more efficient images to improve page load time. We'll look at how to do this in Chapter 11.

In Chapter 12, we'll see how we can customize the CMS user interface, extending it with a custom preview component so that we can see a live preview of how the menu looks from within the CMS.

Finally, in Chapter 13, we'll look at how to leverage Netlify CMS's editorial workflow, creating draft content and reviewing it via GitHub pull requests.

We'll close the book in Chapter 14 with some discussion of Netlify CMS beta features and pointers to more Netlify CMS resources.

CHAPTER 1

Introduction to Netlify CMS

Before we dive into the specifics about Netlify CMS, let's look at a few introductory topics. These include the JAMstack, the Netlify service, and content management systems in general. From there, we'll start looking at Netlify CMS itself.

The JAMstack

Traditional web application stacks such as LAMP (Linux, Apache, MySQL, PHP) or MEAN (MongoDB, Express, Angular, Node.js) specify particular server platforms, programming languages, and database vendors.

JAMstack - that's JavaScript, APIs, and Markup - is a new paradigm for building fast web applications. It is technology-and tool-agnostic. A JAMstack site might be powered by JavaScript via Gatsby or by Ruby via Jekyll.

A JAMstack site pre-renders its pages to static HTML markup which can be served from a CDN or other hosting service. These pages contain JavaScript to provide interactivity, which loads data from an API of some kind. In this model, the application is decoupled from its data.

The API could be a backend service deployed separately, or it could be a third-party service like a headless CMS or a set of AWS Lambda functions.

Figure 1-1 shows an overview of the JAMstack architecture.

1

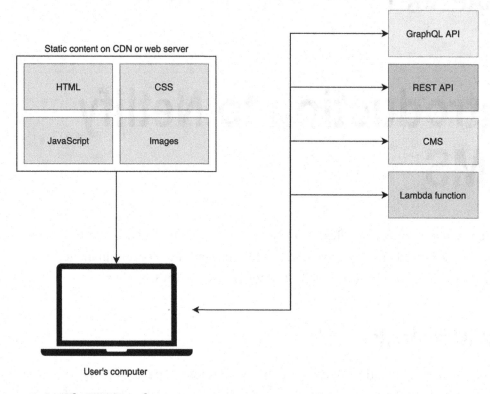

Figure 1-1. *The JAMstack*

One of the biggest benefits of using the JAMstack is performance. Because the pages are generated ahead of time and deployed as static HTML, there is no dynamic generation of HTML from a server and no wait for server-side code to execute. Instead, these static resources can be served from a lightning-fast content delivery network (CDN). By using a CDN, assets are served to a visitor from a server geographically close to them.

There can also be cost savings. Serving your static assets from a CDN is likely less expensive than maintaining your own server infrastructure.

About Netlify

Netlify (https://netlify.com) is a popular platform for hosting websites and applications. At its core, it is a hosting service but also has many other powerful features such as analytics, serverless functions, forms, and a CDN. They have a generous free tier of services.

Netlify's workflow is based on Git repositories. A site is created by connecting a repository from a service like GitHub or GitLab. When a new commit is pushed, Netlify will build and deploy a new version of the site. For this reason, the Netlify platform is well suited to building JAMstack applications.

In this book, we will build and deploy the example project on the Netlify platform.

What is a CMS?

As a web developer, it is easy to build web content by just writing HTML and CSS (or, in the case of Gatsby as we'll see later, Markdown). But consider a nonprofit organization that hires a developer to build a website for them. Unless someone at the nonprofit knows how to code, they will have to spend more money by having the developer come back every time they need the site updated.

A content management system, or CMS, is a solution to this problem. Instead of the content being written in source code, the CMS provides a rich editing experience for authoring and maintaining content. Some features of a CMS might include a WYSIWYG (What You See Is What You Get) editor or a media library for managing images and other media.

A CMS allows multiple authors to draft, edit, and publish content to the site, all without having to worry about writing markup or code. It's also easier because content can be edited directly in the web browser.

A CMS can be used to manage multiple types of content on a site. The most common type of content that comes to mind is an article or blog post. However, a CMS can even be used to provide content on a landing page, header, or footer as well.

Traditional CMS

A traditional CMS is a large web application that handles both the management and display of the content. The content is typically stored in a database of some kind. An author logs in via a web interface, edits the content, and it is saved to the database.

A visitor to the site will utilize the same application to view the content. It retrieves the content from the database where it is presented to the user.

Figure 1-2 shows an overview of a traditional CMS platform.

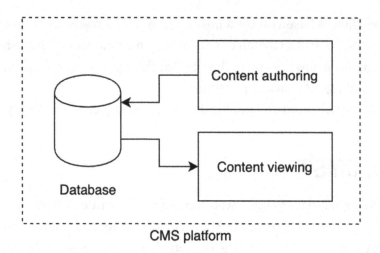

Figure 1-2. *The architecture of a traditional CMS*

Some examples of traditional CMS platforms are WordPress, Drupal, and Joomla.

Headless CMS

A headless CMS is a platform for authoring content but does not contain a front-end interface for displaying that content. Instead, the content is exposed through an API of some kind.

The primary benefit of a headless CMS is that since the content is delivered via an API, it can be consumed by multiple front-end applications. It also provides greater flexibility in how the content is presented. A traditional CMS may be highly customizable, but you are still locked into the platform.

Figure 1-3 shows a typical headless CMS.

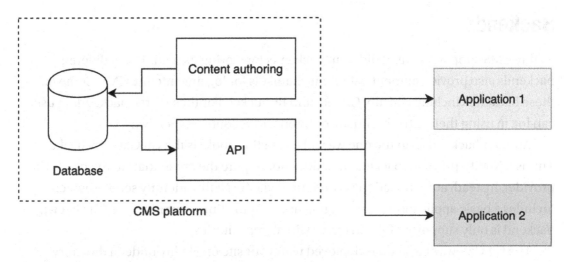

Figure 1-3. *The architecture of a headless CMS platform*

Some examples of headless CMS platforms are Contentful, Magnolia, and Netlify CMS.

As you can probably tell, a headless CMS is a perfect choice for a JAMstack application due to its decoupled, API-first nature. We can build an entire site around the API, using it as a data source for our content.

One potential drawback of a headless CMS is that you may not be able to see a preview of how the content will look on the live site. Fortunately, Netlify CMS supports custom previews, which solves this particular problem.

Netlify CMS

Netlify CMS is a free, open source headless CMS created by Netlify. Despite its name, it is not locked to the Netlify platform. While it is much easier to build and deploy a Netlify CMS-powered site on Netlify, it is not required.

Some CMS platforms store their data in databases that are accessed via an API. Netlify CMS takes a simpler approach. The content is stored as images and Markdown files in a Git repository. This makes it an ideal partner with Gatsby, which has plugins for working directly with, and rendering, Markdown data. It should be noted that Netlify CMS works with other site generators and platforms as well.

Netlify CMS provides a React single-page application with a rich text editor so that content creators don't have to write Markdown directly. While the user interface is powered by React, it can be used with a site built with any technology. Netlify CMS can be used with any platform, such as Hugo, Jekyll, Nuxt, as well as Gatsby.

Backends

Netlify CMS supports several different backends for storing its data. These different backends also provide authentication mechanisms for logging into the CMS. Some of these backends include GitHub, GitLab, and Bitbucket. For these three backends, a user can log in using their GitHub, GitLab, or Bitbucket account, respectively.

Another backend (and the one we will use in this book) is the Git Gateway backend. This is a Netlify-provided backend that does not require the credentials to the user's Git provider. Instead, authentication is configured via the Netlify Identity service, which includes a basic application for managing users. At the time of writing, the Git Gateway backend is only supported for GitHub or GitLab repositories.

The Git Gateway backend is deployed with your site on Netlify under a directory called `.netlify` which contains a basic set of APIs for creating the Git commits. When new content is added, the browser calls these APIs which have some server-side code which will communicate with the configured Git provider's API to create the new Git commit.

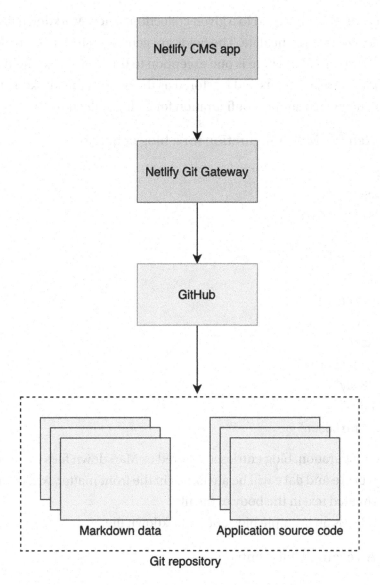

Figure 1-4. *High-level architecture of Netlify CMS*

How it works

Netlify CMS is configured with a YAML file named `config.yml`. This file configures the different resources managed by the CMS. These resources are divided up into *collections*. Each collection will have its own section in the CMS user interface, and each collection defines a set of *fields*. These fields determine which UI controls will appear when editing content in each collection.

When a new resource is added to a given collection, a new Markdown file is created in the repository containing the data. The fields are generally stored as attributes in the Markdown file's front matter. There is one exception to this. If there is a field called body that is of type markdown, it will instead be stored as the body of the Markdown file itself.

Listing 1-1 shows an example configuration for a blog collection.

Listing 1-1. Netlify CMS configuration for a blog collection

```
collections:
  - name: "blog"
  - folder: "src/pages/blog"
  - fields:
    - label: "Title"
      name: "title"
      widget: "string"
    - label: "Publish Date"
      name: "date"
      widget: "datetime"
    - label: "Body"
      name: "body"
      widget: "markdown"
```

With this configuration, blog entries are stored as Markdown files in the src/pages/blog directory. title and date will be attributes in the front matter, while body will be Markdown-formatted text in the body of the file.

Listing 1-2 shows an example blog entry Markdown file.

Listing 1-2. An example blog entry

```
---
title: My First Blog Entry
date: 2020-03-06T02:56:10.463
---
Hello, this is my *first* blog entry.
```

When a new blog entry is created via the CMS, the data will be saved to a new Markdown file under src/pages/blog, and the backend will create a new commit in the site's Git repository, where it is stored along with the application's source code. An updated version of the site is then built and deployed, which will contain the new Markdown file.

Local development

When developing the Gatsby site locally, Netlify CMS is deployed locally into the site, since it is just a React single-page application. However, it works against the remote version of your repository.

This means that if you open the CMS locally and make some changes, those changes won't immediately be reflected in your local copy of the repository. These changes are committed to the remote repository, which will result in the content going live on the deployed site.

In order to access this newly added or modified content locally, you will need to perform a `git pull` operation to pull the new commit from GitHub.

In Netlify CMS 2.10.17, a feature was added that allows you to develop against a local Git repository instead of the live site from the remote repository. This is done by running a local proxy server that Netlify CMS will communicate with, which will create commits in the local Git repository. At the time of writing, however, this feature is still in beta and is subject to change, so we won't cover it here.

For the most up-to-date information, consult the Netlify CMS documentation at `www.netlifycms.org/docs`.

Widgets

The widget types built into Netlify CMS are

- `boolean`: Renders a toggle switch.

- `code`: Renders a code editor with syntax highlighting.

- `datetime`: Renders a date and time picker.

- `file`: Renders a file picker that allows the selection of a file from the media library.

- `hidden`: Does not render a UI control. This widget type can be used for metadata.

- `image`: Similar to `file` but only allows the selection of image files.

- `list`: Can be a list of values or a nested list of fields. Lists can even contain other lists.

- `map`: Renders an interactive map.

- markdown: Renders a rich text editor that stores the data as Markdown.

- number: Renders an input field that only accepts numbers.

- object: Allows grouping of other fields together.

- relation: Used to reference members of a different collection.

- select: Renders a drop-down menu.

- string: Renders a single-line text field.

- text: Renders a multiline text area.

These widgets are assembled into a UI for editing content in the CMS, as shown in Figure 1-5.

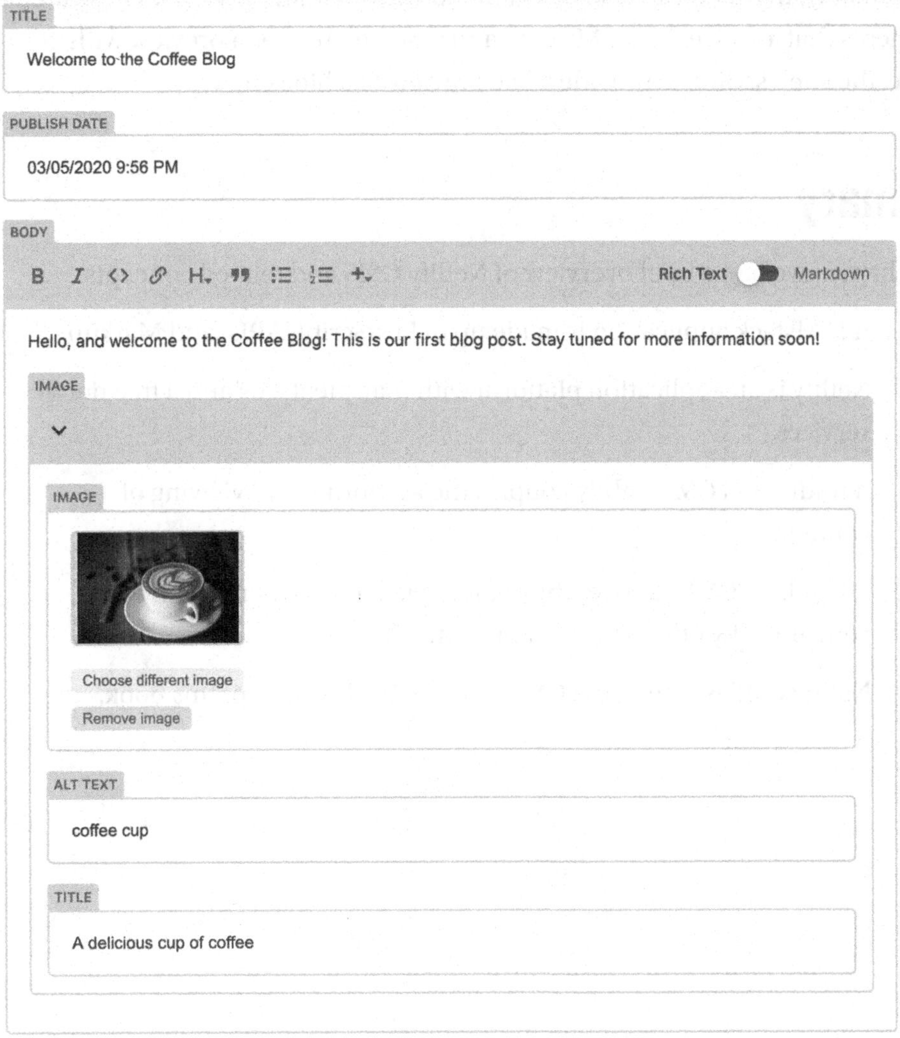

Figure 1-5. *The CMS user interface which is composed of widgets*

If one of the built-in widgets are not suitable for your desired content editing experience, you can create your own. Custom widgets are created as React components and registered with the CMS.

Previews

Netlify CMS shows a live preview of the content being edited. The out-of-the-box experience is very basic, however, and won't be a preview of how the final content will look on the site.

Fortunately, the CMS can also be extended with custom previews. These are React components that are given the CMS data and can then render a preview with, for example, the site's styling to provide a live preview of a blog entry.

Summary

In this chapter, we had a brief overview of Netlify CMS and related concepts:

- A JAMstack application is made up of JavaScript, APIs, and Markup.

- Netlify is an application platform with many features and a free tier of services.

- A traditional CMS tightly couples the authoring and viewing of content.

- A headless CMS exposes the content via an API where it can be consumed by other viewing applications.

- Netlify CMS is a headless CMS that will be the focus of this book.

CHAPTER 2

Gatsby Crash Course

As mentioned in the book's introduction, familiarity with Gatsby is assumed. But, just in case, this chapter will give a quick overview of the basic concepts in Gatsby.

What is Gatsby?

Gatsby (`https://gatsbyjs.org`) is a static site generator for React. Pages are created using React components, then are run through a build process which produces static HTML files and associated assets. These assets can then be deployed to a hosting service like Netlify. Despite the name, a site generated by a static site generator can have dynamic content on the client side. Pages can still contain interactive React components or fetch data over HTTP.

The main difference is, while most React applications are single-page applications (SPAs), Gatsby sites typically have multiple HTML files for different pages.

Creating pages

To create a page in a Gatsby site, you simply create a new React component inside the `src/pages` directory. The file name will determine the URL path to the page. If the file is named `index.js`, then it will be accessed at the root of the site. Otherwise, the URL path to the page is the file name without the `.js` extension. For example, the page `src/pages/about.js` can be accessed at `/about`.

13

© Joe Attardi 2020
J. Attardi, *Using Gatsby and Netlify CMS*, https://doi.org/10.1007/978-1-4842-6297-9_2

GraphQL and Gatsby

GraphQL plays an important role in a Gatsby site. It is a powerful query language that allows you to specify which fields you want returned from the query. With a REST API, the full data set is always returned. GraphQL allows you to get only a subset of the data, as shown in Figure 2-1.

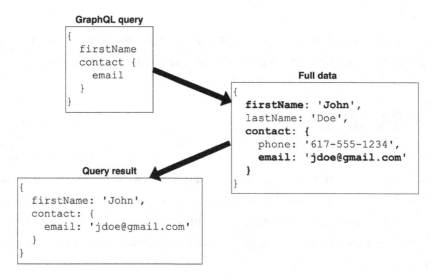

Figure 2-1. *Querying a data structure with GraphQL*

During the build, Gatsby creates a data structure containing all the site's data. What this data structure contains depends on the plugins being used (more on that later). For example, this data structure may contain data about Markdown files discovered during the build, site metadata, or images. To generate site content, Gatsby pages and their associated React components can query this data using GraphQL.

It is important to note that these GraphQL queries are executed at build time, not at runtime.

To define queries, Gatsby provides a *tag* called `graphql`. This tag is used to create tagged templates in the source code: `graphql`Your query here``. This utilizes the template strings feature of JavaScript that was added in ES6. Unlike normal template strings, however, you cannot use the `${}` interpolation syntax as it is not supported for GraphQL queries. During the build process, Gatsby finds these tagged templates, extracts their text content, and builds GraphQL queries with them.

Listing 2-1 shows an example of a simple query to fetch the title of the Gatsby site.

Listing 2-1. A simple Gatsby GraphQL query

```
{
  site {
    siteMetadata {
      title
    }
  }
}
```

The data returned from a GraphQL query has the same structure as the query itself. For example, Listing 2-2 shows the data that would be returned from the query in Listing 2-1.

Listing 2-2. The result of the GraphQL query

```
{
  site: {
    siteMetadata: {
      title: 'My Web Site'
    }
  }
}
```

The GraphiQL tool

Gatsby also ships with a tool called GraphiQL. When the site is running in development mode, the tool can be accessed at http://localhost:8000/___graphql. GraphiQL is a visual development environment for browsing the GraphQL schema, composing queries, and viewing the results. Figure 2-2 shows a screenshot of the GraphiQL tool.

Figure 2-2. *The GraphiQL tool user interface*

On the left is a tree showing the entire schema. Queries can be built interactively by clicking checkboxes next to properties in the schema. In the next panel, the source of the query can be seen, where it can be edited. The third panel shows the result of the query. Lastly, there is also a documentation browser that shows documentation for the different schema elements.

Query types

There are two types of queries in Gatsby.

Page queries

Page queries can only be used in top-level page components. A page query is used by exporting a GraphQL query from the same file as the page component. The result of this GraphQL query is passed to the page as a prop called `data`.

Listing 2-3 has an example of an index page that queries for the site title.

Listing 2-3. A simple page with a page query

```
import React from 'react';
import { graphql } from 'gatsby';

// this is the page
export default function Index({ data }) {
  return (
    <div>
      <h1>Welcome to {data.site.siteMetadata.title}!</h1>
    </div>
  )
}

// this is the page query
export const query = graphql`
  {
    site {
      siteMetadata {
        title
      }
    }
  }
`;
```

Page queries can use variables. Gatsby pages have a concept of a *page context*, which is a way to pass data to dynamically created pages. The properties in this context object can be filled in as variables in a query. We'll see an example of this when we cover dynamic page creation below.

Static queries

Static queries can be used in pages as well as components at any level in the component tree. A static query cannot use variables. Static queries can be used either with the StaticQuery component or with the useStaticQuery hook. These are both provided with Gatsby.

The **StaticQuery** component

Gatsby's StaticQuery executes a GraphQL query, then renders a component, passing the query result to it. It expects two props:

- query: The GraphQL query to execute

- render: A function that takes one argument, the result of the GraphQL query, and returns a React element

Listing 2-4 shows an example component that uses the StaticQuery component.

Listing 2-4. Using StaticQuery

```
import React from 'react';
import { graphql, StaticQuery } from 'gatsby';

export default function SiteTitle() {
  return (
    <StaticQuery
      query={graphql`
        {
          site {
            siteMetadata {
              title
            }
          }
        }
      `}
      render={data => (
        <div>{data.site.siteMetadata.title}</div>
      )} />
  )
}
```

The **useStaticQuery** hook

A newer alternative to the StaticQuery component is the useStaticQuery hook, which can be used inside of a function component. This requires a version of React that supports React Hooks.

To use it, you simply call `useStaticQuery` from inside your function component. Listing 2-5 shows the same component but using `useStaticQuery` instead of `StaticQuery`.

Listing 2-5. Using the `useStaticQuery` hook

```
import React from 'react';
import { graphql, useStaticQuery } from 'gatsby';

export default function SiteTitle() {
  const data = useStaticQuery(graphql`
    {
      site {
        siteMetadata {
          title
        }
      }
    }
  `);

  return <div>{data.site.siteMetadata.title}</div>;
}
```

Plugins

Out of the box, Gatsby doesn't do much. You can create pages from React components and compose your pages using components, but that's about it. Gatsby's real power lies in its plugin ecosystem.

There are many kinds of plugins, but the two we'll focus on here are source plugins and transformer plugins.

Source plugins

Without any plugins, the Gatsby GraphQL schema doesn't have much in it. *Source plugins* add more data from different sources. They gather data from a given source, then call Gatsby's `createNode` function to add it to the GraphQL schema.

In our example project, we will use the `gatsby-source-filesystem` plugin. This plugin adds data about files in the local filesystem. Given a source directory, it will create new GraphQL nodes for each file.

There are many other source plugins, for different APIs, content management systems, and more. They all fetch data from some data source and add that data to the GraphQL schema. There are source plugins for CMS platforms such as Contentful or WordPress, as well as sources for services such as Shopify (for building ecommerce sites) or even for pulling files directly from a Git repository.

Transformer plugins

Transformer plugins take the data from source plugins and transform them into something more useful. For example, suppose you have a directory full of Markdown files you want to use for blog posts. The first step is to use the `gatsby-source-filesystem` plugin to add the Markdown files to the GraphQL schema.

However, this doesn't expose the content of the Markdown files. For this, you can use the `gatsby-transformer-remark` plugin. This plugin reads the Markdown files and exposes the metadata in the front matter (Front matter is a block of metadata at the beginning of a Markdown file). It also uses Remark, a Markdown processing library, to transform the Markdown source into rendered HTML.

Like source plugins, the `gatsby-transformer-remark` plugin adds new nodes to the GraphQL schema containing the front matter metadata and rendered HTML. For example, all of the Markdown files that were found are accessible in a query via the `allMarkdownRemark` field. An example query is shown in Listing 2-6.

Listing 2-6. An example query using `gatsby-transformer-remark`

```
query BlogQuery {
  allMarkdownRemark {
    edges {
      node {
        html
        frontmatter {
          title
        }
      }
    }
  }
}
```

You might be wondering what the edges and node fields are in the query. The allMarkdownRemark field is known as a *connection*. This is a type that represents a group of nodes of a given type. The conceptual model of GraphQL is that of a graph, so you can think of it as a node with edges connecting it to other nodes, as visualized in Figure 2-3.

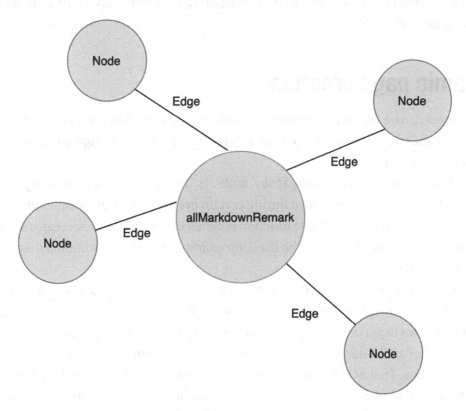

Figure 2-3. *GraphQL edges and nodes*

The allMarkdownRemark field has an edge field, which is the set of edges shown in Figure 2-3. Each of the edges has a node field, which is connected to the actual data.

Some other examples of transformer plugins are gatsby-transformer-json, which transforms data from a JSON source, and gatbsy-transformer-yaml, which transforms data from a YAML source. In all, there are over 145 different transformer plugins available in the Gatsby plugin ecosystem.

Other plugins

Besides source and transformer plugins, there are other types of Gatsby plugins as well. These include `gatsby-plugin-netlify-cms`, which integrates the Netlify CMS user interface with the Gatsby site, and `gatsby-plugin-sass`, which allows Sass style sheets to be used instead of CSS.

Dynamic page creation

Gatsby pages can be added by creating new files in the `pages` directory. These pages are defined ahead of time. But for our site to work, we'll need to configure Gatsby to dynamically create pages.

This is done with a special file, `gatsby-node.js`. This file provides the ability to implement functions that are called during certain events in the Gatsby build process.

For example, the `onCreateNode` function is called every time Gatsby creates a node in the GraphQL structure. This could be used, for example, to define additional metadata on some created nodes.

Pages are dynamically created by implementing the `createPages` function. Gatsby calls this function after the GraphQL schema is created. Because of this, you can execute GraphQL queries to get data that can be used to dynamically create pages.

The `createPages` function is passed as an object with some helper objects, one of which is `actions`. That `actions` object contains, among other things, a helper function called `createPage`. To create a page, this function is called with the desired URL path, the component to use for the page, and the page context, where we can add custom data.

This context data can then be passed into variables in the page's GraphQL query. For example, you might query for all blog entries via `allMarkdownRemark`, then call `createPage` for each of the returned entries, passing the slug (identifying portion of the page URL) of the Markdown data to the context, as shown in Listing 2-7.

Listing 2-7. Dynamically creating a page

```
blogEntries.forEach(({ node }) => {
  createPage({
    path: node.fields.slug,
    component: path.resolve('./src/templates/blog.js'),
    context: {
```

```
        slug: node.fields.slug
      }
    });
  });
```

The code in Listing 2-7 calls `createPage` for each blog entry that was found. The React component found in the file `./src/templates/blog.js` will be used to render the page, and the slug will be passed to the page's context, which will then be used in a query variable of the same name, as shown in Listing 2-8.

Listing 2-8. A page query that uses a variable, passed in via the context

```
export const query = graphql`
  query($slug: String!) {
    markdownRemark(fields: { slug: { eq: $slug } }) {
      html
      frontmatter {
        title
      }
    }
  }
`;
```

Markdown primer

Netlify CMS publishes its content as Markdown files. Gatsby reads and parses those files to render the content using the `gatsby-transformer-remark` plugin. Because we're using the CMS, we won't have to write Markdown directly. But in case you haven't been exposed to it before, here's a quick introduction.

Markdown is a lightweight language for formatting text, created in 2004. It uses plain text files with a very simple set of symbols for formatting. Usually, the Markdown is run through a parsing and rendering process to output HTML.

Basic formatting

There are varying "flavors" of Markdown, but here is some of the common formatting syntax:

- Headings: A heading is preceded by one or more pound sign characters (#). The heading level is determined by the number of pound signs. # is heading 1, ## is heading 2, etc.

- Paragraphs: Paragraphs are separated by blank lines.

- Bold: Text is made bold by putting either two asterisks (**) or underscores (__) at the beginning and end of a string. For example, `**I'm bold**` or `__I'm bold__`.

- Italic: Text is made italic by putting either a single asterisk (*) or underscore (_) at the beginning and end of a string. For example, `*I'm italic*` or `_I'm italic_`.

- Unordered lists: One item per line, preceded by either an asterisk or dash. For example:

  ```
  - Item One
  - Item Two
  ```

- Ordered lists: One item per line, preceded by a number, starting with 1. For example:

  ```
  1. Item One
  2. Item Two
  ```

- Links: Links follow the format `[Link text](Link URL)`.

Front matter

Some tools, such as Gatsby, support the embedding of metadata in a Markdown file This is done in a special section at the beginning of the file called the *front matter*. This section contains key/value pairs, with the key and value separated by a colon. The front matter begins and ends with three dashes on their own line.

Listing 2-9 shows an example of a Markdown file with front matter.

Listing 2-9. Markdown with front matter

```
---
title: "Shopping List"
author: "John Doe"
---

# Shopping List

Here are some items I need to pick up at the grocery store.

- milk
- eggs
- cheese
```

Gatsby starters

You could set up a Gatsby site from scratch if you wanted to. But there are many Gatsby *starters* that already exist. These are templates for different types of Gatsby sites. They are hosted on GitHub, and a new site can be created by running the command `gatsby new <site name> <URL of starter>`.

Our example project was created with the most minimal starter, called `gatsby-starter-hello-world`. There are many other popular starters that you could use to create a Gatsby site, such as

- `gatsby-starter-blog`: A basic blog.

- `gatsby-starter-default`: A basic starter with a few predefined pages.

- `gatsby-starter-deck`: Create presentations powered by Gatsby.

For a full list of starters, visit `www.gatsbyjs.org/starters`.

The build process

The Gatsby build process goes through several steps to transform your source code into static assets ready to be deployed. Here are the main high-level steps that are performed.

Data model and GraphQL schema creation

First, Gatsby builds its internal data model. This is the data that we can query with GraphQL in our pages and components. What this data model looks like depends on what plugins are configured for the site. This is where source and transformer plugins are executed, adding nodes to the data.

Once the data model is created, the GraphQL schema is built. This is the schema against which queries are validated.

Page creation

Once the data model is created, dynamic page creation takes place, calling the `createPages` function if it is defined in `gatsby-node.js`.

Query extraction

Gatsby now searches for GraphQL queries. It does this by creating an abstract syntax tree (AST) of the JavaScript files and looking for templates tagged with `graphql`. The queries are compiled, and if any of them contain a syntax error, the build process fails.

Query execution

Now the queries are actually executed against the data. First, static queries are executed, followed by page queries. The resulting data is passed to the page and non-page components for the next step.

Static HTML generation

Here is where Gatsby differs from a traditional React application. In a typical React application, the user interface is built completely at runtime in the browser using React. The only HTML that comes from the server is a shell page containing an empty element where the generated markup will be inserted. The UI is not visible until (1) the JavaScript files are downloaded and (2) the JavaScript code is executed to build the UI. This can sometimes have a performance penalty.

Gatsby performs a static render of the React components. This means that as part of the build process, React code runs that generates the HTML markup. This markup is saved to static HTML files. When a visitor loads a page on a Gatsby site, the full HTML of the page is served to the client.

Of course, a static HTML page is not very useful, especially if you want to create an interactive application. This is where the process of *hydration* comes in.

When a visitor loads the page, since the HTML has already been generated, it appears very quickly. In the meantime, the JavaScript code for the interactive portions of the page are being loaded. Once the JavaScript is available, React takes control of the page. Event listeners are added, and state is injected into the components. After the hydration process completes, the static page has been transformed into a full-blown React application.

Summary

In this chapter, we took a high-level look at Gatsby, its concepts, and its build process:

- Gatsby is a static site generator for React.

- Gatsby uses GraphQL for its data model. Pages and components perform GraphQL queries to retrieve their necessary data.

- Gatsby has a rich plugin ecosystem, including source plugins and transformer plugins.

- Plugins add data to the site's GraphQL schema.

- Markdown is a simple markup language for formatting text, which Gatsby and Netlify CMS use for data.

- Static HTML is generated at build time; later, hydration is used to transform the page into an interactive React application.

CHAPTER 3

Setting Up the Example Project

Throughout this book, we will build a website for a coffee shop using Gatsby and Netlify CMS. It will include an index page, a menu, and a blog. We will deploy the site on Netlify via GitHub.

Prerequisites

Before we can set up the project, there are a few prerequisite steps required.

Install Git

To work with the example project and deploy it to Netlify, you will need to have Git installed on your system. Installation steps vary depending on your operating system. See `https://git-scm.com/` to download and install Git.

If your operating system has a package manager, chances are there is a Git package for it. If you're on a Mac or Linux system, Git may already be installed.

Install Node.js

To install dependencies and run the build process, you will need Node.js installed on your system. If you don't have it installed already, you can download it from `https://nodejs.org`. You can download either the current or LTS (long-term support) version - either will work for this project.

Installing Node.js will also install the npm package manager tool, which we'll use to install dependencies.

© Joe Attardi 2020
J. Attardi, *Using Gatsby and Netlify CMS*, https://doi.org/10.1007/978-1-4842-6297-9_3

Install the Gatsby command line interface

The Gatsby command line interface, or CLI, is how we interact with Gatsby. It can create new projects, run a development server, or build the final artifacts to deploy a site. The CLI is published as an npm package called `gatsby-cli`. To install it, open a terminal and run the following command:

```
npm install -g gatsby-cli
```

The `-g` argument to the `npm install` command installs the gatsby-cli package globally. After the package is installed, the gatsby command will be available on your system.

Sign up for GitHub

We will deploy the project to Netlify via GitHub, and the starter code is stored there, so you'll need a GitHub account if you don't already have one. To sign up, you can go to `https://github.com/join`.

Create a new repository with the starter code

You won't need to start from scratch for this project. There is a GitHub template repository with the starter code that you can use to create your own repository to work in.

The starter code is located at `https://github.com/joeattardi/coffee-shop-starter`. To set up your repository, visit this URL. Make sure you are logged in to your GitHub account, then click the green "Use this template" button, as shown in the screenshot in Figure 3-1.

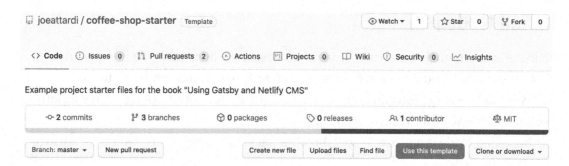

Figure 3-1. *The starter code repository*

When you click this button, you will be prompted for the desired name of your repository. Enter something like "coffee-shop" and click "Create repository from template."

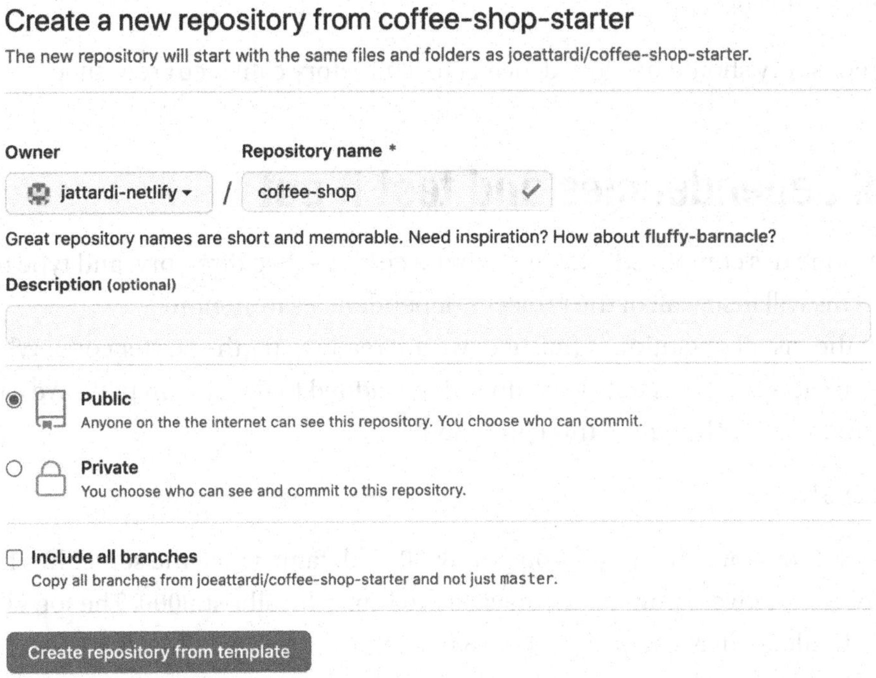

Figure 3-2. *Creating the new repository*

Clone the repository

After a brief delay, you will be taken to your new repository page. From this page, click the green "Clone or download" button, then click the clipboard icon to copy the URL to your clipboard.

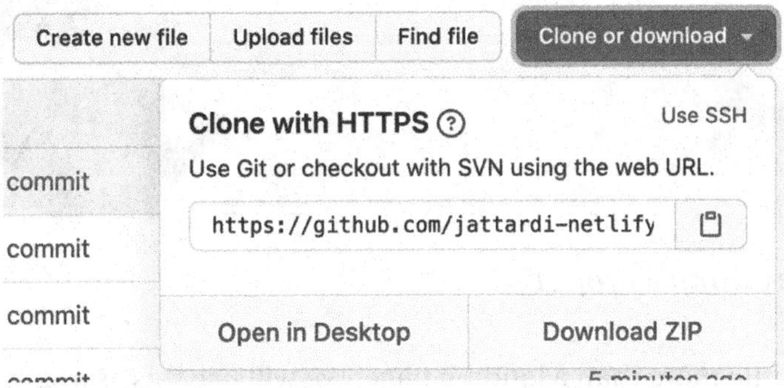

Figure 3-3. *Getting the clone URL for your repository*

Now, we can clone the repository to our system. From the terminal, change into the directory that you want the code to be stored in, then type this command:

```
git clone <your URL>
```

The repository should be cloned locally to a directory called `coffee-shop`.

Install dependencies and test it out

Once the clone has completed, change into the `coffee-shop` directory, and type `npm install`. This will install all of the project's dependencies from npm.

When the install operation is finished, we are ready to try the starter code. When we installed the Gatsby CLI, a `gatsby` command was added to the system path. We can start a development server by typing this command:

```
gatsby develop
```

The development server listens on port 8000 by default. Once the server has finished starting, open your web browser and navigate to http://localhost:8000. The Joe's Coffee Shop site should load. A screenshot is shown in Figure 3-4.

Figure 3-4.   *The example project*

So far, this is little more than a landing page. We will use this as a starting point and will add functionality to the site over the next several chapters.

Deploy on Netlify

The next step is to get the example project deployed on Netlify.

Sign up

If you don't already have a Netlify account, we will set one up in this section and link it to our GitHub account. Feel free to skip the sign-up section if you already have an account linked to GitHub.

Open your browser and go to `https://netlify.com`, and click the "Sign up" link. You will be prompted to select a sign-up method, as shown in Figure 3-5.

Figure 3-5. *Selecting a sign-up method*

Click the "GitHub" button to continue. You will then be redirected to GitHub, where you will be prompted to authorize Netlify. Click the green "Authorize netlify" button, shown in Figure 3-6, to complete the sign-up process.

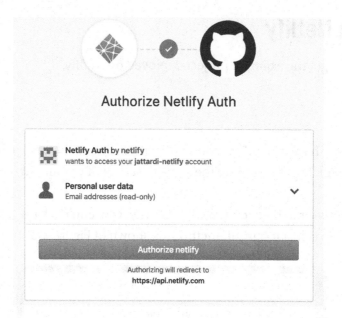

Figure 3-6. *Authorizing Netlify with GitHub*

You will then be redirected to the Netlify dashboard, where you will be logged in, as shown in Figure 3-7.

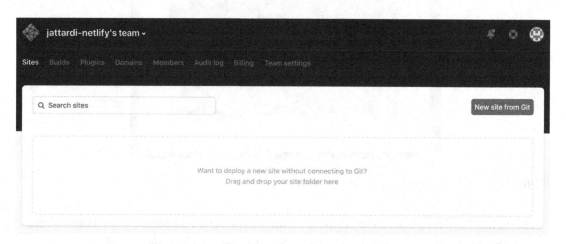

Figure 3-7. *The Netlify dashboard*

Create a new site

Next, we'll create a new site for the example project and point it at our GitHub repository. From the dashboard, click the "New site from Git" button. Under "Continuous Deployment," click the "GitHub" button.

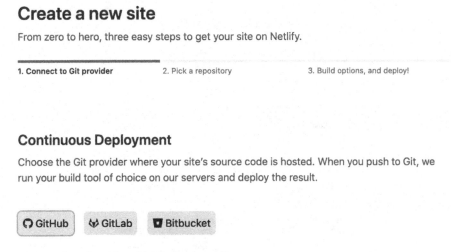

Figure 3-8. *Selecting the GitHub provider*

You will again be redirected to GitHub, where you will be prompted to give Netlify permission to access your repositories. Click the green "Authorize Netlify by Netlify" button.

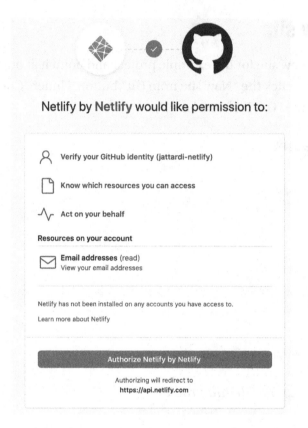

Figure 3-9. *Authorizing Netlify*

Once you have authorized Netlify, you will be prompted to install the Netlify GitHub app on your account. You can grant Netlify access to all of your repositories or just the coffee-shop repository, if you prefer.

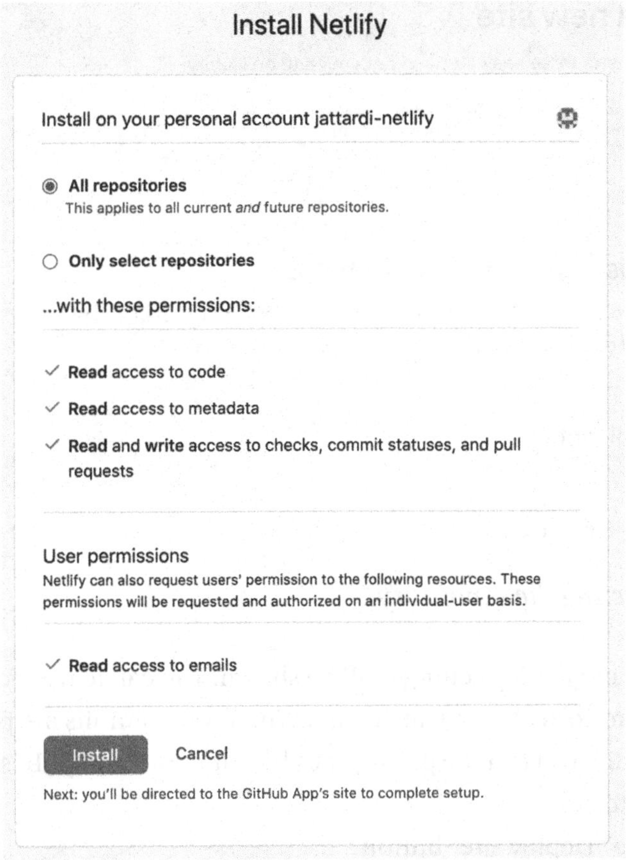

Install Netlify

Install on your personal account jattardi-netlify

◉ **All repositories**
   This applies to all current *and* future repositories.

○ **Only select repositories**

...with these permissions:

✓ **Read** access to code

✓ **Read** access to metadata

✓ **Read** and **write** access to checks, commit statuses, and pull requests

User permissions
Netlify can also request users' permission to the following resources. These permissions will be requested and authorized on an individual-user basis.

✓ **Read** access to emails

[Install]   Cancel

Next: you'll be directed to the GitHub App's site to complete setup.

Figure 3-10. *Installing the Netlify app*

Once the app is installed, you will be redirected back to Netlify, where you will be prompted to choose which repository to use for the new site. Click the `coffee-shop` repository.

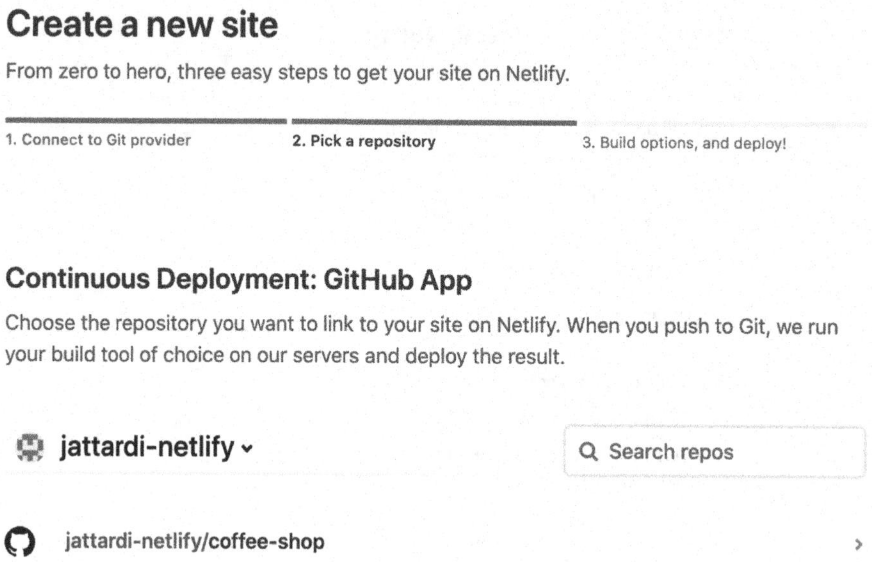

Create a new site

From zero to hero, three easy steps to get your site on Netlify.

1. Connect to Git provider   **2. Pick a repository**   3. Build options, and deploy!

Continuous Deployment: GitHub App

Choose the repository you want to link to your site on Netlify. When you push to Git, we run your build tool of choice on our servers and deploy the result.

🎮 **jattardi-netlify** ˅

Q Search repos

⭕ **jattardi-netlify/coffee-shop**   ›

Figure 3-11. *Selecting the repository*

Next, the build and deploy settings will be shown. You can leave the defaults selected, as these are correct for a Gatsby site. Whenever commits are pushed to the `master` branch, Netlify will run the `gatsby build` command and publish the files that go in the `public` directory.

Finally, click the "Deploy site" button.

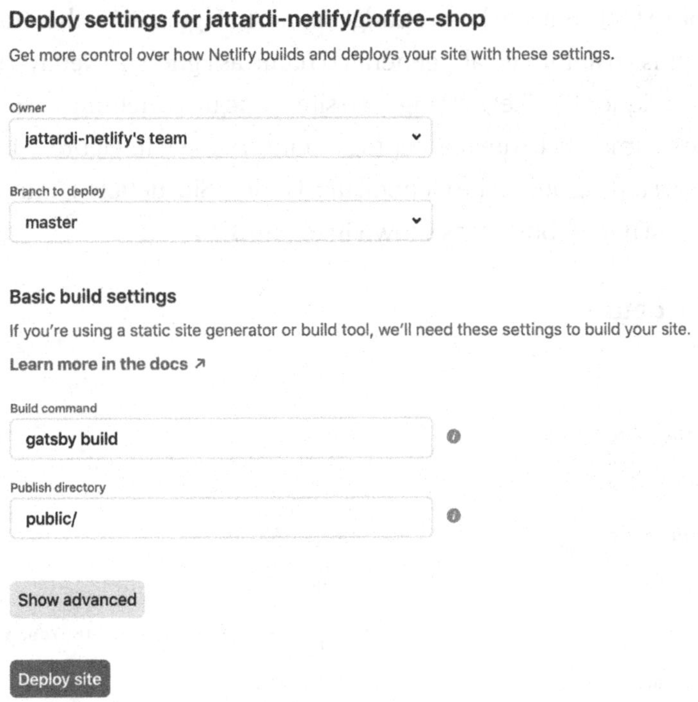

Deploy settings for jattardi-netlify/coffee-shop

Get more control over how Netlify builds and deploys your site with these settings.

Owner

jattardi-netlify's team ⌄

Branch to deploy

master ⌄

Basic build settings

If you're using a static site generator or build tool, we'll need these settings to build your site.

Learn more in the docs ↗

Build command

gatsby build   ⓘ

Publish directory

public/   ⓘ

Show advanced

Deploy site

Figure 3-12. *The site deploy settings*

You will be taken to the overview page for the new site, with a status of "Site deploy in progress," as shown in Figure 3-13.

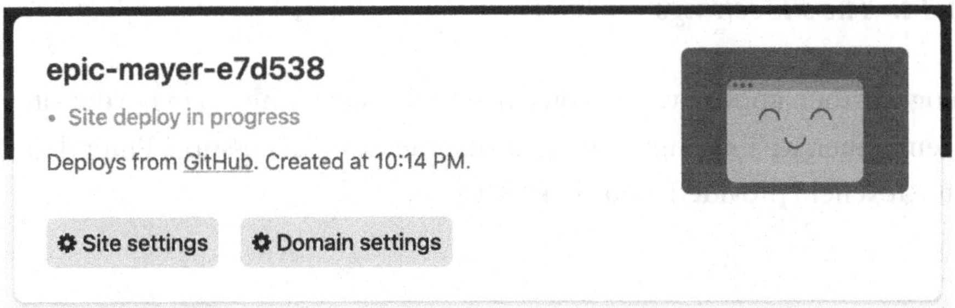

epic-mayer-e7d538

• Site deploy in progress

Deploys from <u>GitHub</u>. Created at 10:14 PM.

⚙ Site settings   ⚙ Domain settings

Figure 3-13. *Site deploy in progress*

You might notice that your site has a strange name. In Figure 3-13, the site name is epic-mayer-e7d538. This is an automatically generated name assigned by Netlify to your site, to make sure it has a unique URL. Let's change the site name to something easier to remember. To change the site's name, click the "Site settings" button shown in Figure 3-13. The site settings will appear, starting out in the General tab. Under "Site details": "Site information," click the "Change site name" button, as shown in Figure 3-14.

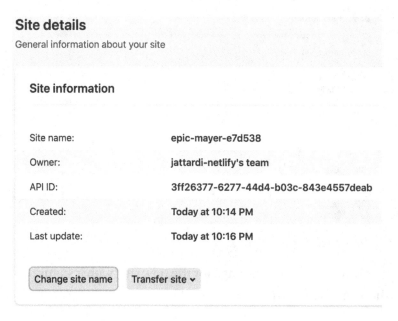

Figure 3-14. *The site settings*

A dialog will then appear, where you can edit the site name. To make the site name easier to remember, we'll change it to <your-username>-coffee-shop. Enter that new site name in the text field provided, and click "Save."

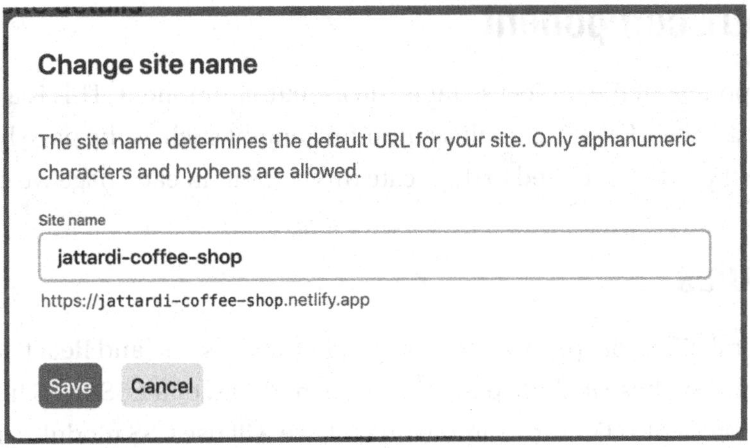

Change site name

The site name determines the default URL for your site. Only alphanumeric
characters and hyphens are allowed.

Site name

jattardi-coffee-shop

https://jattardi-coffee-shop.netlify.app

Save   Cancel

Figure 3-15. *Changing the site name*

Finally, let's try out the live site. In the browser, navigate to https://<your-username>-
coffee-shop.netlify.app, and the landing page should appear. We have successfully
deployed the project to Netlify. In the future, any time we push commits to the master
branch in GitHub, Netlify will build and deploy the new version of the site here.

A tour of the example project

So far, the example project is little more than a landing page. It was created with the
gatsby-starter-hello-world Gatsby starter, which is a template for creating new
Gatsby sites. Initially, there are no plugins installed in our site. Throughout this book,
however, we will install several Gatsby plugins.

Directory structure

There are just a few directories:

- src: Source files.

- src/components: Reusable components, used by pages.

- src/pages: The site's pages. For now, there is just an index page.

- static: Static resources such as images.

The Layout component

The only component in the project so far is the Layout component. This is a common pattern in Gatsby sites. Layout contains common content such as the page header and title. This is so that we don't need to duplicate this content in each page we create.

CSS modules

There are several different approaches to styling in Gatsby sites (and React applications in general). Some of these include plain CSS, CSS modules, or a CSS-in-JS framework like styled-components. For the example project, we will use CSS modules, mostly to keep things simple.

Each component or page will have a corresponding CSS module file. For example, the Layout component in Layout.js has its styles defined in Layout.module.css. In a CSS module file, you define CSS rules like you usually do in a style sheet. Listing 3-1 shows a simple example CSS module file, Sample.module.css.

Listing 3-1. A simple CSS module

```
.header {
  background: red;
}
.footer {
  background: blue;
}
```

A CSS module is imported into a JavaScript file. The class names from the CSS are exported from the CSS module, which can be used by the component that imports it. This is demonstrated in Listing 3-2, the source code for the corresponding component, Sample.js.

Listing 3-2. Consuming a CSS module

```
import styles from './Sample.module.css';
```

```
export default function Sample() {
  return (
    <div>
      <header className={styles.header}>Header</header>
      <footer className={styles.footer}>Footer</footer>
    </div>
  );
}
```

The class names used by the elements in the Sample component are not strings but rather references to the exported class names. This is an important distinction, because when the final CSS is built, there will be no selectors for the classes header or footer.

Instead, these class names will have a unique identifier added to them to effectively scope the styles to the component. The exports from the CSS module provide a mapping between the class name in the source CSS and the generated class names at build time.

For example, the header class selector will be rendered as something like Sample-module–header–3zaAq. The HTML rendered by the React component will also reference these generated class names. This ensures that the styles in the CSS module will only apply to the React component importing it.

Without CSS modules, style rules could apply to other parts of the page outside of the component, producing unintended effects.

Special Gatsby files

The project also contains some special Gatsby files:

- gatsby-browser.js: An entry point to utilize the Gatsby Browser APIs. Here, we simply use it to import a style sheet containing some global styles.

- gatsby-config.js: The main Gatsby configuration file. Here is where plugins are configured.

So far, the site's configuration is pretty bare bones. It currently only contains the site name, as shown in Listing 3-3.

Listing 3-3. The initial Gatsby configuration

```
module.exports = {
  siteMetadata: {
    title: 'The Coffee Blog'
  }
};
```

Summary

In this chapter, we

- Installed required tools

- Set up our development environment

- Created our project repository from the starter code

- Deployed the initial project to Netlify

We also took a brief look at the initial project code and got an introduction to CSS Modules.

CHAPTER 4

Setting Up Netlify CMS

Let's dive right in and start building the coffee shop site. The first step is to install and configure Netlify CMS and integrate it with Gatsby.

Install dependencies

We first need to install a few packages from npm:

- `netlify-cms-app`: The Netlify CMS application itself

- `gatsby-plugin-netlify-cms`: The Netlify CMS Gatsby plugin

Open a terminal, go to the project directory, and type the command to install these packages. Note that we are installing specific versions. This is because by default, npm installs the latest version of a package, and there may be later breaking changes that do not work with the example project in this book. To prevent this, it is best to install specific versions:

```
npm install netlify-cms-app@2.12.15 \
            gatsby-plugin-netlify-cms@4.3.5
```

Configuration

Netlify CMS is configured with a YAML file named `config.yml`.

© Joe Attardi 2020
J. Attardi, *Using Gatsby and Netlify CMS*, https://doi.org/10.1007/978-1-4842-6297-9_4

YAML primer

YAML, short for *YAML Ain't Markup Language* (a recursive acronym!), is a commonly used configuration file format. The Netlify CMS configuration file is a set of key/value pairs, also known as a dictionary. The value can be a scalar value (string, number, boolean, and so on), another dictionary, or an array.

Keys and values in a dictionary are separated by a colon, as shown in Listing 4-1.

Listing 4-1. A simple YAML dictionary

```
name: Joe
email: jattardi@gmail.com
```

Dictionaries can also be specified on a single line with curly braces, as shown in Listing 4-2.

Listing 4-2. A single-line YAML dictionary

```
{ name: 'Joe', email: 'jattardi@gmail.com' }
```

An array is a sequence of values. Each item of an array begins with a dash character on its own line, followed by the value (which may take up multiple lines). Listing 4-3 is an example of an array.

Listing 4-3. A YAML array

```
- name: Joe Attardi
  email: jattardi@gmail.com
- name: John Doe
  email: jdoe@gmail.com
- name: Jane Doe
  email: janedoe@gmail.com
```

In more complex structures, there can be arrays of dictionaries, dictionaries of arrays, or a combination of both, as shown in Listing 4-4.

Listing 4-4. A more complex YAML structure

```
name: John Doe
contact:
```

```
  - type: email,
    value: jdoe@gmail.com
  - type: phone,
    value: 617-555-1234
skills:
  - javascript
  - html
```

Creating the initial configuration

Inside the `static` directory, create a new directory called `admin`. Inside that directory, create the configuration file, `config.yml`. Finally, inside the configuration file, add the initial configuration, shown in Listing 4-5.

Listing 4-5. The initial CMS configuration

```
backend:
  name: git-gateway
  branch: master

media_folder: static/img
public_folder: /img
```

Let's go over this configuration. First, we configure the Netlify CMS backend. There are several supported backends, but we are using the Git Gateway backend. This is a generic backend that uses our Git repository as the data store and Netlify Identity for authentication to the CMS application.

The `media_folder` option is the path on disk that static media resources will be kept. When a user uploads new images via the CMS, they will be saved to this directory. When the image `cat.gif` is uploaded, it will be stored as `static/img/cat.gif` in the repository.

The `public_folder` option is the URL, relative to the Gatsby site's root, that the images will be served from. When running the site locally, for example, cat.gif will be served from http://localhost:8000/img/cat.gif.

Now we need some content for our CMS to manage. The site will have a blog, so let's look at collections and set up a blog collection.

Collections

All pieces of content managed by Netlify CMS are members of a collection. Collections are configured in the `config.yml` file. There are a few different types of collections.

Folder collections

A folder collection represents content items in a common format, stored under a common folder. New items can be added to a folder collection via the UI. All files under the given folder will be part of the folder collection and are expected to have a consistent structure.

A folder collection is configured by setting a `folder` property in the collection configuration. We will use a folder collection for the blog posts.

Filtered folder collections

It is possible to have varied files under the same folder by using filtered folder collections. Like folder collections, the content files are all located under one folder, but you can specify filter criteria to only select certain files in that folder.

Like folder collections, a filtered folder collection needs to have a `folder` property that specifies the common containing folder. Additionally, there is a `filter` property that specifies criteria. Only files matching the criteria will be included in the filtered folder collection. An example filter criteria is `{ field: "language", value: "en" }`. This collection will only include files with a language of en.

File collections

While folder collections are general-purpose collections that can contain arbitrary files, a file collection explicitly defines specific files that should be part of that collection. Only those files will be included in the collection. To set up a file collection, the collection configuration should have a `files` property that is an array of files.

A file collection would be used for defining pages of a site that can have dynamically managed content, for example, a Home or About page.

Configuring the blog collection

Let's add our first collection. In `config.yml`, create a collections section and fill it in as shown in Listing 4-6.

Listing 4-6. Configuration for the blog collection

```
collections:
  - name: "blog"
    label: "Blog"
    folder: "src/blog"
    create: true
    slug: "{{year}}-{{month}}-{{day}}-{{slug}}"
    fields:
      - label: "Title"
        name: "title"
        widget: "string"
      - label: "Publish Date"
        name: "date"
        widget: "datetime"
      - label: "Body"
        name: "body"
        widget: "markdown"
```

First, we give the collection a `name`. This is the name that the collection will be referred to by internally. The `label` property specifies the display name in the UI for this collection.

The `folder` property sets the root folder where the blog posts will reside, relative to the project root.

The `create` property determines whether or not new items can be created in this collection using the CMS application.

Next is the `slug` property, which defines the pattern to use for constructing the slugs of blog posts. A slug is a URL-friendly, human-readable version of a string. Each blog post's URL will contain this configured slug. An example slug for a blog post might look like this: `2020-06-20-hello-world`. Blog post titles will be turned into slugs when creating pages for the posts. For example, the blog post title "Here's Blog Post #2!" might have a slug of `heres-blog-post-2`.

Lastly, we configure the `fields` for this collection. We will keep it simple here. Each blog post has a title, publish date, and a body. Each field has a widget type specified. This determines the UI control that is used for editing that value in the CMS application.

More about fields

By default, fields are required. Netlify CMS will not allow an entry to be published unless all required fields have a value. A field can be marked as optional by specifying a `required: false` option in the collection's configuration.

Fields also support basic validation. You can specify a `pattern` property. The value of this property should be an array. The first element of the array is a regular expression string, and the second element is the error message to display if the input doesn't match the regular expression.

Blog posts will be stored as Markdown files. Each field is set as a property in the front matter, except for the `body` field. When Netlify CMS sees a `body` field with a widget type of `markdown`, it stores that field as the main body of the Markdown file rather than inside the front matter.

Listing 4-7 shows what an example blog post in this collection might look like.

Listing 4-7. An example blog post

```
---
title: Hello World!
date: "2020-03-05T22:40:32.169Z"
---

Hello World! This is my first blog post.
```

Add the Gatsby plugin

The last step is to configure the Gatsby plugin. Open the `gatsby-config.js` file in the root of the project. Add a `plugins` section with a single plugin, `gatsby-plugin-netlify-cms`, as shown in Listing 4-8.

Listing 4-8. Updated Gatsby configuration

```
module.exports = {
  siteMetadata: {
    title: 'The Coffee Blog'
  },

  plugins: [
    'gatsby-plugin-netlify-cms'
  ]
};
```

Commit and deploy

Before we can use the Netlify CMS application to add a blog post, we need to deploy a new version of the site which contains the `config.yml` file and the Netlify CMS application itself. Let's pause here, make a commit, and push to GitHub.

```
git add .
git commit -m "Add initial configuration"
git push origin master
```

After a moment, Netlify will see that you pushed to the `master` branch and will build and deploy the new version of the site.

Configure Netlify Identity and Git Gateway

The last thing to do before we can add a new blog post is to configure Netlify Identity and Git Gateway. Netlify Identity is a built-in basic identity provider that administrators of your site can use to log in and use the CMS to add and manage content.

To do this, you'll need to log in to your Netlify account. Once you've done this, click your site to go to the site dashboard. Then, click "Site settings." This will load your site settings screen. On the left side of the screen, click the "Identity" link. Netlify Identity is not currently enabled, so you should see a button labeled "Enable Identity." Click that button to begin.

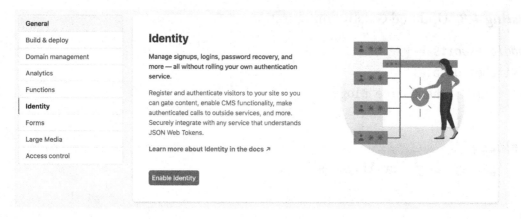

Figure 4-1. *The Identity tab*

Once you click the button, Identity will be enabled immediately, and you'll be presented with the Identity settings screen. Click the "Registration" link. For now, we'll use open registration for convenience.

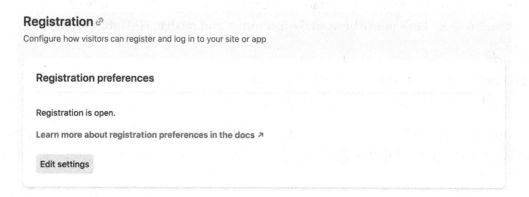

Figure 4-2. *Open registration enabled*

Next, we'll enable Git Gateway for the site. Click the "Services" link on the left under "Identity," and click the "Enable Git Gateway" button.

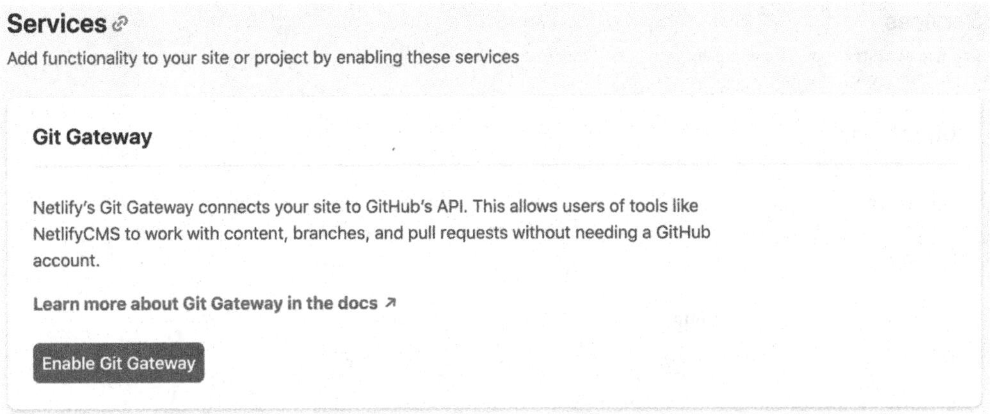

Services
Add functionality to your site or project by enabling these services
Git Gateway
Netlify's Git Gateway connects your site to GitHub's API. This allows users of tools like NetlifyCMS to work with content, branches, and pull requests without needing a GitHub account.
Learn more about Git Gateway in the docs
Enable Git Gateway

Figure 4-3. *Enabling Git Gateway*

After clicking the button, a new window will pop up prompting you to grant additional permissions to Netlify Auth. Click the "Authorize netlify" button.

Netlify Auth is requesting additional permissions
Netlify Auth by netlify
would like additional permissions to
Repositories
Public and private
Existing access
Access user email addresses (read-only)
Authorize netlify
Authorizing will redirect to
https://api.netlify.com

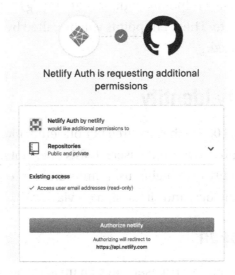

Figure 4-4. *Granting additional permissions*

After you grant these permissions, you will be redirected back to the Netlify settings page, where you will see that Git Gateway has been enabled.

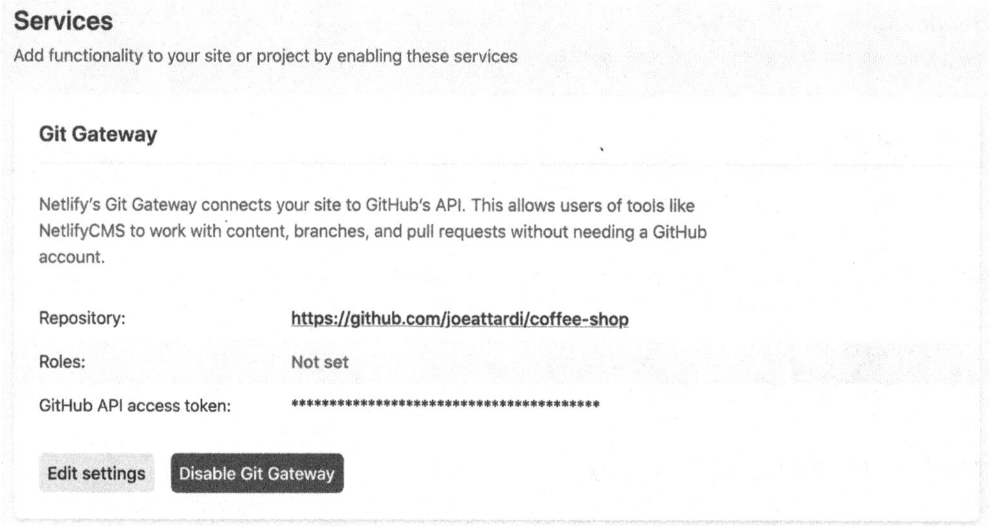

Figure 4-5. *Git Gateway enabled*

Git Gateway adds several endpoints under /.netlify/git/github that act as a proxy to GitHub's API from our site. These endpoints will be called by the CMS when content is added, modified, or removed.

More about Netlify Identity

We are using Identity Level 0, which is the free tier of Netlify Identity. With that, you get up to 1,000 active users and 5 invite-only users. If this does not meet your needs, there are also paid levels of Identity with higher user limits and more features such as custom branded log-in pages, audit logs, and single sign on via SAML.

Invite-only registration

We configured open registration, so a user can sign up at the log-in screen of the CMS. You can also set registration to invite-only. In this configuration, you can invite users via the Netlify Identity settings UI, and users will not be able to sign themselves up.

To enable invite-only registration, from the Settings page, go to "Identity": "Registration," and click "Edit". A form will be displayed where you can change the registration to be invite-only.

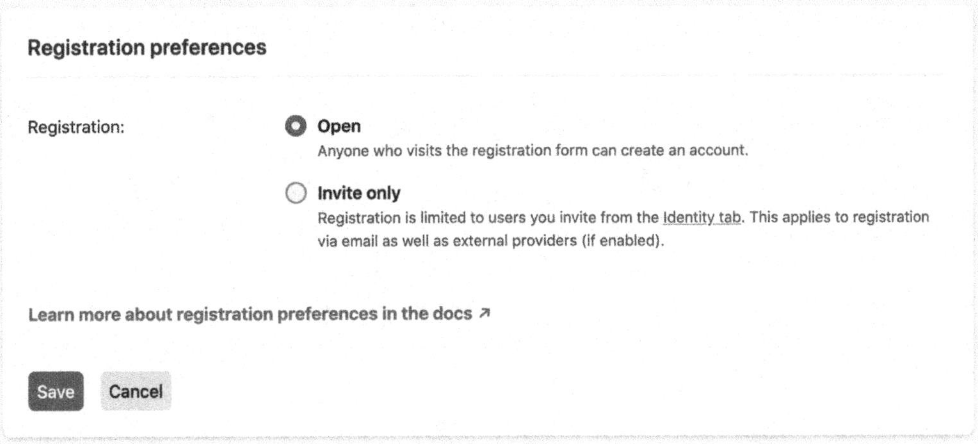

Registration preferences

Registration: ⦿ **Open**
                         Anyone who visits the registration form can create an account.

                       ◯ **Invite only**
                         Registration is limited to users you invite from the Identity tab. This applies to registration
                         via email as well as external providers (if enabled).

Learn more about registration preferences in the docs ↗

Save   Cancel

Figure 4-6. *Editing registration preferences for Netlify Identity*

Summary

In this chapter, we

- Installed Netlify CMS and the Netlify CMS Gatsby plugin

- Configured the blog collection

- Enabled Netlify Identity and Git Gateway

CHAPTER 5

The Netlify CMS Application

We've installed and configured Netlify CMS, but how do we add posts to our blog? That's where the Netlify CMS application comes in. When we installed the Netlify CMS Gatsby plugin, it configured a route in the Gatsby site, `/admin`, which will load the CMS user interface so that we can manage content.

Registering and logging in

To get started, open a web browser and go to the live version of the site at https://<your-site-name>.netlify.app/admin. You will see the Netlify CMS logo and a log-in button, as shown in Figure 5-1.

Figure 5-1. *The log-in screen*

Click the "Login with Netlify Identity" button. A dialog will appear with two tabs: "Sign up" and "Log in." Since we configured Netlify Identity to use open registration, we can sign up here for a new user account. Click the "Sign up" tab. Enter your name and email, and select a password, then click "Sign up."

57

© Joe Attardi 2020
J. Attardi, *Using Gatsby and Netlify CMS*, https://doi.org/10.1007/978-1-4842-6297-9_5

Figure 5-2. *Signing up for a new account*

After clicking the "Sign up" button, you will receive an email from Netlify to confirm your email address. Click the link in this email to complete the sign-up process. Once this is complete, you will be redirected to the main screen of the Netlify CMS Content Manager application. There isn't much to see here yet, since we haven't added any blog posts.

Figure 5-3. *The Netlify CMS application*

On the left side of the screen is the list of collections. So far, we only have one collection, the Blog collection. The name that is displayed here is determined by the value of the label property in the collection configuration. As more collections are added, they will appear in this list.

Once we have created some blog posts, they will be listed in the center region. Currently it says "No Entries" because no posts have been created yet.

In the top right part of the screen is the "Quick add" button. This allows you to start the content creation process from any screen in the application.

Lastly, in the top left are two buttons: "Contents" and "Media." This is used to switch between the main view and the media asset manager, which we will look at soon.

Creating a new blog post

Now that we're logged in, let's create a new blog post. In the center region of the screen, click the "New Blog" button. This will open a new editor where we can add the new blog post, as shown in Figure 5-4.

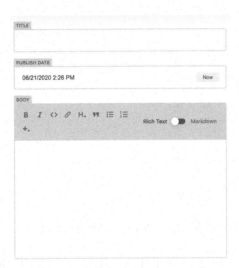

Figure 5-4. *The CMS editing interface*

There are three fields shown in this editor: *Title*, *Publish Date*, and *Body*. These correspond to the three fields we configured in the CMS configuration file for the blog collection.

Let's add a new post. First, enter a title in the Title field. The widget used for the Title field is string, which renders a single-line text field, as shown in Figure 5-5.

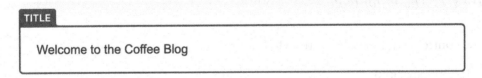

Figure 5-5. *The editor for the Title field editing interface*

Next, let's look at the Publish Date field. It has been prefilled with the current date and time. Click the field, and a date and time picker will appear.

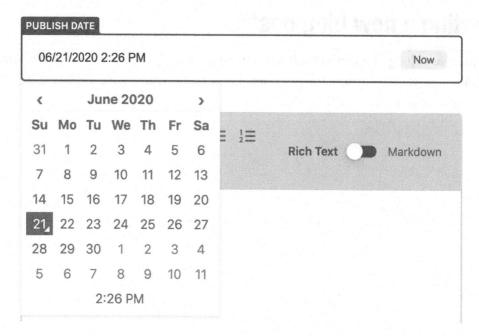

Figure 5-6. *The date picker for the Publish Date field*

For now, we can leave the date and time as is. Lastly, let's add some content to the blog post. The Body field has a rich text editor. Figure 5-7 shows the different toolbar buttons that are available for formatting the text.

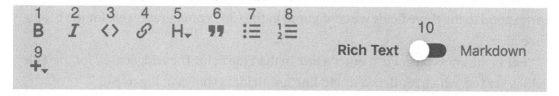

Figure 5-7. *The editor toolbar*

The controls on the toolbar are as follows:

1. Toggles bold.

2. Toggles italic.

3. Toggles code/monospaced font.

4. Inserts a hyperlink.

5. Sets the heading style. There are six available heading levels.

6. Inserts a block quote.

7. Inserts an unordered list.

8. Inserts an ordered list.

9. Adds content to the text. Currently, the available options are images and code blocks.

10. Toggles between the formatted text and the Markdown source.

Go ahead and type a blog post in the Body field, using the various toolbar controls to format the text.

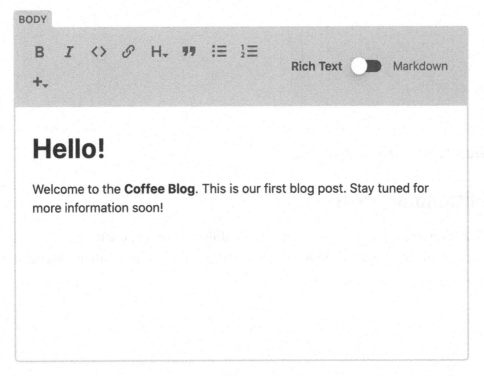

Figure 5-8. Some content added to the Body field

If you prefer, you can also edit the raw Markdown source itself. To do this, simply click the toggle switch from "Rich Text" to "Markdown." The content will transform into Markdown-formatted text.

Figure 5-9. *The Markdown source*

Publishing the post

Finally, let's publish this new post. Click the "Publish" button in the top right corner of the screen. This will open a dropdown menu with a few options. From this menu, click "Publish now."

Figure 5-10. *The publish menu*

After a brief delay, the top of the screen will change to indicate that the new post was saved and published. The "Publish" button in the top right has changed to say "Published."

Let's return to the main screen of the CMS. To do this, click the back button in the upper left corner of the screen.

Figure 5-11. *The back button*

Back at the main screen, you will now see the blog post we just added. It should look like Figure 5-12.

Figure 5-12. *The main screen showing the newly published blog post*

How publishing works

We are using the Git Gateway backend, connected to GitHub. When we clicked the "Publish" button, here's what happened:

- A Markdown document was created for the blog post, containing the metadata in the front matter and the content in the body.

- Using the GitHub API via the Git Gateway, a new commit was created containing this document on the `master` branch.

- Since a new commit was created on the `master` branch, Netlify built and published a new version of the site containing the new blog post.

To see this, from the terminal, perform a `git pull` operation:

```
git pull origin master
```

You will see one new commit downloaded from GitHub. If you check the `src` directory, you'll see a new directory called `blog`. Inside that directory is a new file. The filename should look something like `2020-06-21-welcome-to-the-coffee-blog.md`. This filename is generated from the configuration file. Recall that for the `blog` collection, we set the slug pattern to `{{year}}-{{month}}-{{day}}-{{slug}}`.

If you open the new Markdown file in your editor, it will look something like what is shown in Listing 5-1.

Listing 5-1. The Markdown file that was generated by the CMS

```
---
title: Welcome to the Coffee Blog
date: 2020-06-21T18:26:40.185Z
---
# Hello!

Welcome to the **Coffee Blog**. This is our first blog post. Stay tuned for
more information soon!
```

Adding media

The Netlify CMS application also includes an interface for managing media files. You can upload images and other media here.

To access the media manager, click the "Media" button at the top of the page.

Figure 5-13. *The toolbar containing the "Media" button*

We haven't added any media yet, so the media manager will be empty, as shown in Figure 5-14.

Figure 5-14. *The empty media manager*

Let's upload an image to add to our blog post. Open up your favorite image search engine and find an image of a cup of coffee, then save it to your computer.

Then, in the media manager, click the "Upload" button. Select the image that you downloaded in the file chooser that appears, and it will be added to your media library. This is done by using the Git Gateway to create a new commit in the repository containing the image – media files are also stored in the repository.

After uploading, the media manager will refresh, and you will see the new coffee image, as shown in Figure 5-15.

Figure 5-15. *The new image in the media manager*

Alternative media storage options

As with the site content, all media is stored in your Git repository. After you upload an image, a new commit will be created in the repository which adds that image.

If your site has lots of media files, or large ones like audio and video, the Git repository can become quite large. Netlify CMS supports several solutions to this problem:

- Cloudinary (`https://cloudinary.com`) and Uploadcare (`https://uploadcare.com`) are third-party CDNs for managing and distributing media content. Netlify CMS has native support for working with these services.

- Netlify Large Media is another service offered by Netlify. It is a Git LFS (Large File Storage) service. Note that this service requires hosting your site on the Netlify platform.

Adding media to a blog post

Let's add the image we just uploaded to the blog post we created previously. Click the X to close the media manager, then click the blog post in the list of content.

Inserting the image

Go to the beginning of the body content, then click the plus button on the toolbar. You will see the Add menu pop up, as shown in Figure 5-16.

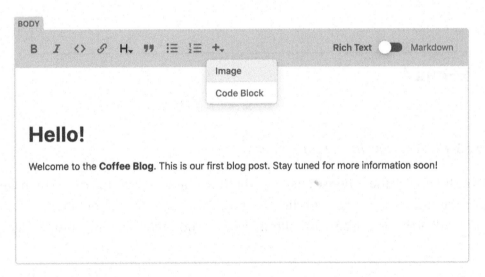

Figure 5-16. *The Add toolbar menu*

From the pop-up menu, click "Image." This will add an image component to the text editor.

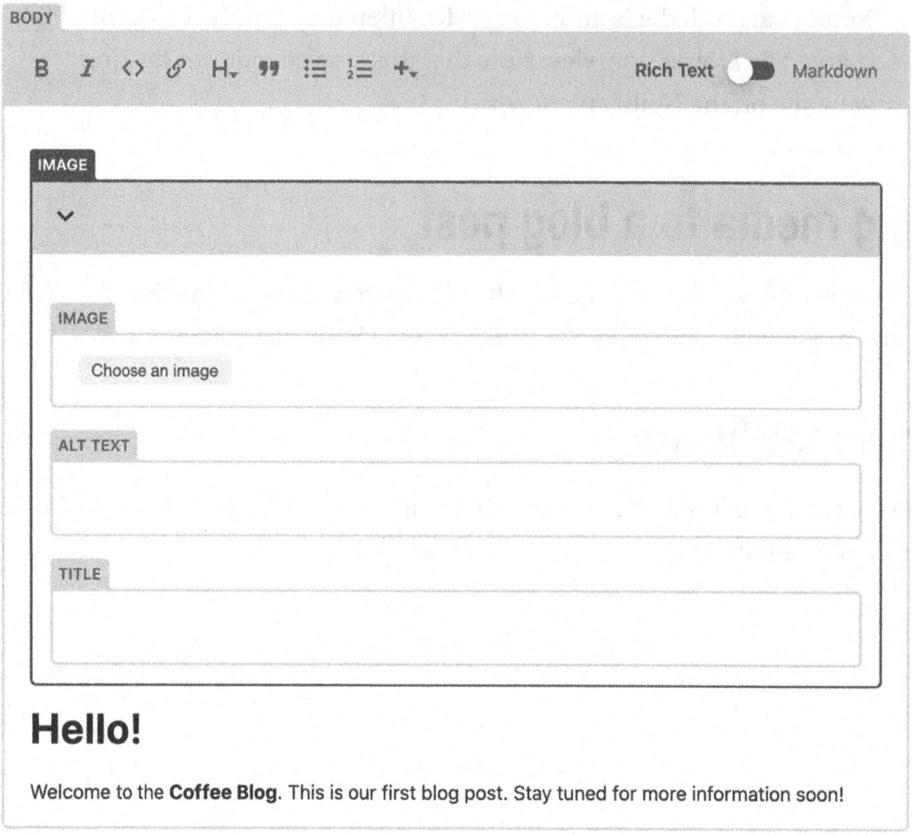

Figure 5-17. *The new image component*

From here, click the "Choose an image" button. This will show the media manager. Click on the coffee cup image, and click the green "Choose selected" button in the top right of the dialog. You can also add alternative text and a title (tooltip) for the image.

Figure 5-18. *The editor with an image added*

Publishing the updated blog post

The last step to update the blog entry is to republish it. As we did before, click "Publish," then click "Publish now." Once the updated blog post is published, Netlify will begin deploying the new version of the site containing the updated blog post.

While this is happening, go back to your terminal and perform another `git pull` operation:

```
git pull origin master
```

You will see that the blog post file was updated and a new file was added in the `static/img` directory. This is what we configured for the `media_folder` option in the CMS configuration file.

Summary

In this chapter, we

- Created an account in the CMS application

- Created and published a new blog post

- Added an image to the blog post

CHAPTER 6

Sourcing Blog Data

Gatsby is extremely flexible and customizable. As mentioned in Chapter 2, one of the features of Gatsby is that it can dynamically create pages from data. In this chapter, we'll install some plugins and write some JavaScript code in our Gatsby site to load the blog post data and create a list of entries on the main page.

Gatsby plugin configuration

Gatsby plugins are configured in the main configuration file, `gatsby-config.js`. This file contains a `plugins` array. Each element of the `plugins` array can be either a simple string specifying the name of a plugin (in which case it will use the default settings for that plugin) or an object containing two properties:

- resolve: The name of the plugin

- options: Any options to be passed to the plugin

Making Gatsby aware of the Markdown files

The first step is to make Gatsby aware of the Markdown files that are generated by Netlify CMS. For this, we'll need to install the `gatsby-source-filesystem` plugin. The first step, as always, is to install the package. Open a terminal and run the following command:

```
npm install gatsby-source-filesystem@2.3.14
```

Next, let's configure the plugin. Open the file `gatsby-config.js,` and add a new entry to the `plugins` array, as shown in Listing 6-1.

© Joe Attardi 2020
J. Attardi, *Using Gatsby and Netlify CMS*, https://doi.org/10.1007/978-1-4842-6297-9_6

Listing 6-1. The updated Gatsby configuration file

```
module.exports = {
  siteMetadata: {
    title: 'The Coffee Blog'
  },

  plugins: [
    'gatsby-plugin-netlify-cms',
    {
      resolve: 'gatsby-source-filesystem',
      options: {
        name: 'blog',
        path: 'src/blog'
      }
    }
  ]
};
```

This plugin will add some new nodes to the GraphQL schema for our site. Specifically, an `allFile` node will be added that will let you query files found in the `src/blog` directory. With this plugin, you can run queries like the one shown in Listing 6-2.

Listing 6-2. Example filesystem query

```
{
  allFile {
    edges {
      node {
        extension
        dir
        modifiedTime
      }
    }
  }
}
```

Or you can query for specific files, like in Listing 6-3.

Listing 6-3. Querying for a specific file

```
{
  allFile(filter: { name: { eq: "2020-03-06-welcome-to-the-coffee-blog" }
}) {
    edges {
      node {
        extension
        dir
        modifiedTime
      }
    }
  }
}
```

Parsing the Markdown data

Once we are loading the files with `gatsby-source-filesystem`, we want to parse the Markdown data and front matter and add this information to the GraphQL schema. For that, we use the `gatsby-transformer-remark` plugin.

Remark is a Markdown processor for JavaScript. It takes Markdown source and renders it as HTML markup. We will use this HTML markup in our Gatsby site to present blog entries. It can also parse a Markdown file's front matter.

First, let's install the package. Run the following command:

```
npm install gatsby-transformer-remark@2.8.19
```

Then, as before, we need to configure Gatsby to use this plugin. The plugin itself doesn't need any configuration - the defaults are sufficient for our use case. We just need to add another entry to our plugins array in `gatsby-config.js`. Open the file, and add the code indicated in Listing 6-4.

Listing 6-4. Adding the gatsby-transformer-remark plugin

```
module.exports = {
  siteMetadata: {
    title: 'The Coffee Blog'
  },
```

73

```
  plugins: [
    'gatsby-plugin-netlify-cms',
    {
      resolve: 'gatsby-source-filesystem',
      options: {
        name: 'blog',
        path: 'src/blog'
      }
    },
    'gatsby-transformer-remark'
  ]
};
```

With `gatsby-transformer-remark`, we can (among other things) convert the Markdown syntax to its equivalent HTML markup with a query like the one shown in Listing 6-5.

Listing 6-5. An example query

```
{
  allMarkdownRemark {
    edges {
      node {
        html
      }
    }
  }
}
```

This query will give us the Markdown data rendered as HTML, ready to insert into a React component for display to the user.

Querying and displaying the data

Now that we've installed the necessary plugins, let's continue on and try to display our blog post in the example project.

Creating a blog post component

First, we'll create a React component that will display an excerpt of a single blog post. This component will later be used in the index page, which will list all of the blog posts. Create a new file in src/components called BlogPost.js. Add the code from Listing 6-6.

Listing 6-6. The BlogPost component

```
import React from 'react';

import styles from './BlogPost.module.css';

export default function BlogPost({ title, date, excerpt }) {
  return (
    <article className={styles.blog}>
      <h2>{title}</h2>
      <h3>{date}</h3>
      <p>{excerpt}</p>
    </article>
  );
}
```

This is a simple presentational component that receives all of its data as props passed from a parent component. It then simply renders the data that was passed to it. In this file, we are also importing a CSS module. Let's create that next. Create the file src/components/BlogPost.module.css, as shown in Listing 6-7.

Listing 6-7. The CSS module for the BlogPost component

```
.blog {
  padding: 1rem;
}

.blog h2 {
  margin: 0;
}
```

```
.blog h3 {
  margin: 0;
  font-style: italic;
}
```

Creating a blog list component and querying for data

Next, we'll create a BlogList component that will contain a GraphQL query for the blog data. Create a new file src/components/BlogList.js, as shown in Listing 6-8.

Listing 6-8. The BlogList component

```
import React from 'react';

import { graphql, useStaticQuery } from 'gatsby';

import BlogPost from './BlogPost;

export default function BlogList() {
  const data = useStaticQuery(graphql`
    {
      allMarkdownRemark {
        edges {
          node {
            id
            frontmatter {
              title
              date(formatString: "MMMM D, YYYY")
            }
            excerpt
          }
        }
      }
    }
  `);
```

```
  return (
    <div>
      {data.allMarkdownRemark.edges.map(edge => (
        <BlogPost
          key={edge.node.id}
          title={edge.node.frontmatter.title}
          date={edge.node.frontmatter.date}
          excerpt={edge.node.excerpt} />
      ))}
    </div>
  );
}
```

In this component, we are using the useStaticQuery hook that comes with Gatsby. We are querying for the Markdown data. The frontmatter field contains all front matter data, and the excerpt field contains an excerpt containing, by default, the first 140 characters of the blog post's body. By default, this excerpt is returned as plain text, but it can also be returned as HTML if desired.

Using the BlogList component

Finally, we need to use the BlogList component from the index page. Change the file src/pages/index.js to match Listing 6-9.

Listing 6-9. Adding the BlogList component

```
import React from 'react';

import { graphql, useStaticQuery } from 'gatsby';

import BlogList from '../components/BlogList';
import Layout from '../components/Layout';

import styles from './index.module.css';

export default function IndexPage() {
  const data = useStaticQuery(graphql`
```

```
    {
      site {
        siteMetadata {
          title
        }
      }
    }
  `);

  return (
    <Layout>
      <div id={styles.hero}>
        <h1>{data.site.siteMetadata.title}</h1>
      </div>
      <BlogList />
    </Layout>
  );
}
```

Let's try the `BlogList` and `BlogPost` components in the site and see how they are working. From the project directory, run the command:

```
gatsby develop
```

This will start the Gatsby development server, which we will use heavily throughout this book to test our changes. Once you see the message "You can now view gatsby-starter-hello-world in the browser," open your browser and go to http://localhost:8000. You should see the index page, including the blog post that we added earlier, as shown in Figure 6-1.

Figure 6-1. *The blog post is now on the index page*

Now that we have verified that the new code is working, let's create a new commit and push to GitHub. Run the following commands:

```
git add .
git commit -m "Add initial blog post listing"
git push origin master
```

Once you push the code, Netlify will notice the new commit and start a new build of the site. After a few minutes, the new version of the site containing the blog list will be live.

Adding a second blog post

So far, we only have a single blog post. Let's add a second post so that we can see a listing of multiple posts. Once Netlify has deployed the new version of the site, go to https://<your-site-name>.netlify.app/admin. Log in if prompted and use the CMS application to add a second blog post.

After publishing the new post, we will need to pull down the new commit containing the second post. From the terminal, run this command:

```
git pull origin master
```

You should get one new commit containing the new blog post's Markdown file. Rerun `gatsby develop`, and go to http://localhost:8000 again. There should be two blog posts listed now, as shown in Figure 6-2.

Figure 6-2. *The second blog post appears in the blog list*

Fixing the sort order

You might have noticed that the blog posts are out of order. Typically, in a blog, the newest posts are shown at the top. Currently, that is not the case. We can fix this by specifying a sort order in the GraphQL query.

Open the file src/components/BlogList.js, and change the GraphQL query as shown in Listing 6-10.

Listing 6-10. Adding a sort order to the GraphQL query

```
import React from 'react';

import { graphql, useStaticQuery } from 'gatsby';

import BlogPost from './BlogPost';

export default function BlogList() {
  const data = useStaticQuery(graphql`
    {
      allMarkdownRemark(sort: { fields: frontmatter___date, order: DESC })
{
        edges {
          node {
            id
            frontmatter {
              title
              date(formatString: "MMMM D, YYYY")
            }
            excerpt
          }
        }
      }
    }
  `);

  return (
    <div>
```

```
    {data.allMarkdownRemark.edges.map(edge => (
      <BlogPost
        key={edge.node.id}
        title={edge.node.frontmatter.title}
        date={edge.node.frontmatter.date}
        excerpt={edge.node.excerpt}
      />
    ))}
  </div>
  );
}
```

We are telling GraphQL to sort the returned Markdown files in descending order of the date property in their front matter. If we reload the index page, we can see that the blog posts are now sorted correctly.

Let's commit and push this fix.

```
git add .
git commit -m "Sort blog posts by date"
git push origin master
```

Second Blog Post
June 26, 2020

This is the second blog post!

Welcome to the Coffee Blog
June 21, 2020

coffee cup Hello! Welcome to the Coffee Blog. This is our first blog post. Stay tuned for more information soon!

Figure 6-3. *The blog posts in the correct order*

Summary

In this chapter, we

- Used a source plugin to load the Netlify CMS Markdown files

- Used a transformer plugin to parse the Markdown and front matter

- Added a list of blog posts to the index page of the example project

CHAPTER 7

Dynamic Page Creation

Our home page shows a listing of all the blog posts, which displays excerpts, but we still need a dedicated page for each post to show their full content. By hooking into Gatsby's APIs, we can dynamically create pages based on the blog post data.

Gatsby Node APIs

First, create a new file in the root of the project called `gatsby-node.js`. This is a special file that is used to implement the Gatsby Node APIs. It allows you to manipulate and query the GraphQL data and create pages based on that data.

The various functions in this file are called at different times during the build process. Here are two of these functions that we will use in the example project.

onCreateNode

This function is called whenever a new node is created in the Gatsby data structure. For example, this function will be called once for each of our Markdown files since they are nodes created by the `gatsby-source-filesystem` plugin we configured earlier.

We will use `onCreateNode` to create *slugs* for our blog posts. As mentioned earlier, a slug is a human-readable, URL-friendly representation of the blog post title. The slug is used to register the blog post page URL and to create links to blog posts from the index page.

`onCreateNode` is called with an object containing the node being created and an `actions` object that contains several functions that can be called to perform different actions.

© Joe Attardi 2020
J. Attardi, *Using Gatsby and Netlify CMS*, https://doi.org/10.1007/978-1-4842-6297-9_7

createPages

After data is sourced by source plugins and transformed by transformer plugins, this function is called to give us an opportunity to dynamically create pages. Because the data model has been built before this function is called, we can run GraphQL queries to look up the data we need to create our pages.

We will create a template page that will have data passed to it, which will result in a unique page for each blog post.

createPages is called with an object containing a graphql function for querying the data and an actions object similar to the one passed to onCreateNode.

Adding the slug to the blog post data

When new blog posts are added, we will get the slug for each post and add it as a new *field* on the blog post data. Later, we'll use this slug field to create the URLs for the blog post pages. The slug is based on the filename of the Markdown file.

Open the newly created gatsby-node.js file and add the code in Listing 7-1. This code is taken from the code in the Gatsby tutorial, which can be found at www.gatsbyjs. org/tutorial/part-seven/#creating-slugs-for-pages.

Listing 7-1. Adding the slug

```
const { createFilePath } = require('gatsby-source-filesystem');

exports.onCreateNode = function({ node, getNode, actions }) {
  const { createNodeField } = actions;

  if (node.internal.type === 'MarkdownRemark') {
    const slug = createFilePath({ node, getNode });
    createNodeField({
      node,
      name: 'slug',
      value: slug
    });
  }
};
```

First, we require a helper function, createFilePath, from the gatsby-source-filesystem plugin. This function creates a URL from a file's path.

Next, we implement the onCreateNode function. The argument to this function is destructured to get the node, a helper function called getNode, and an actions object containing some other actions that can be performed on the node.

We then destructure the actions object and pull out the createNodeField function, which is used to add additional fields to a node. These new fields are added under a field called fields.

This function gets called whenever a node of any type is created. We only want to perform this action when the node being created represents a Markdown file, so we check if the node's type is MarkdownRemark. If it is, then we use createFilePath to generate the slug for the file.

Finally, we call createNodeField to add the slug field to the node.

We can now query for the slug field as shown in Listing 7-2.

Listing 7-2. Querying for the slug field

```
{
  allMarkdownRemark {
    edges {
      node {
        fields {
          slug
        }
      }
    }
  }
}
```

Dynamically creating the blog post pages

Next, we'll tap into Gatsby's createPages API to dynamically create blog post pages. First, we'll create a *template* page that will be used as a base for the dynamically created pages. Then, we'll perform a GraphQL query for the slugs of all the blog posts.

Each slug will be passed as a context parameter to the template page, which will be used in the template's page query to query for the full blog post data and render it.

The process is outlined in Figure 7-1.

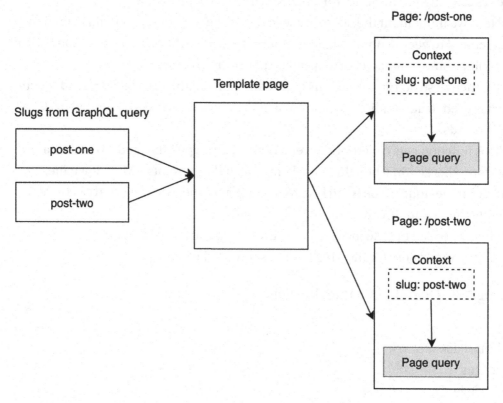

Figure 7-1. *Creating pages from a template*

Creating the blog post template

Create a new directory `src/templates` and create a new file inside that directory called `blog.js`. Enter the contents of Listing 7-3.

Listing 7-3. The blog post page template

```
import React from 'react';

import { graphql } from 'gatsby';

import Layout from '../components/Layout';

import styles from './blog.module.css';
```

```
export default function BlogTemplate({ data }) {
  return (
    <Layout>
      <div className={styles.blog}>
        <h1>{data.markdownRemark.frontmatter.title}</h1>
        <div dangerouslySetInnerHTML={{ __html: data.markdownRemark.html }} />
      </div>
    </Layout>
  );
}

export const query = graphql`
  query($slug: String!) {
    markdownRemark(fields: { slug: { eq: $slug } }) {
      html
      frontmatter {
        title
      }
    }
  }
`;
```

The file's default export, as usual, is the React component for the template page. There's also a named export called query. This is the page query. The exported query will be executed by Gatsby when building the site. Note that the query takes a $slug parameter. This will receive the slug context parameter in the createPages function we'll write next.

The slug is passed as an argument to the markdownRemark query to look up the specific blog post. We're querying for the rendered HTML and the title from the front matter.

The page component receives the result of the GraphQL query as the data prop. We then use the values in the data prop to populate the blog post page. In particular, we use React's dangerouslySetInnerHTML to set the rendered HTML from Remark as the inner HTML of the element.

Next, let's create a quick CSS module for the template page. Create a file `src/templates/blog.module.css` and add the code from Listing 7-4.

Listing 7-4. Simple CSS module for the blog template page

```css
.blog {
  padding: 1rem;
}

.blog h1 {
  margin: 0;
}
```

Creating the pages

Now that we've created the template, we'll use the `createPages` API to generate the blog post pages. Open the file `gatsby-node.js` and add the `createPages` function as shown in Listing 7-5. This code is taken from the code in the Gatsby tutorial, which can be found at www.gatsbyjs.org/tutorial/part-seven/#creating-pages.

Listing 7-5. The updated `gatsby-node.js`

```js
const path = require('path');

const { createFilePath } = require('gatsby-source-filesystem');

exports.onCreateNode = function({ node, getNode, actions }) {
  const { createNodeField } = actions;

  if (node.internal.type === 'MarkdownRemark') {
    const slug = createFilePath({ node, getNode });
    createNodeField({
      node,
      name: 'slug',
      value: slug
    });
  }
};
```

```
exports.createPages = async function({ graphql, actions }) {
  const { createPage } = actions;

  const result = await graphql(`
    query {
      allMarkdownRemark {
        edges {
          node {
            fields {
              slug
            }
          }
        }
      }
    }
  `);

  result.data.allMarkdownRemark.edges
    .forEach(({ node }) => {
      createPage({
        path: node.fields.slug,
        component: path
          .resolve('./src/templates/blog.js'),
        context: {
          slug: node.fields.slug
        }
      });
    });
};
```

We've added the Gatsby createPages API to this file. As with onCreateNode, there is an actions property that contains various helper functions. We use destructuring to access the createPage action. Next, we perform a GraphQL query to find the slugs of all of the blog posts.

Note that this GraphQL query looks a little different than other queries we've seen so far. Earlier, we saw queries defined using the graphql tag on a template string. Here, graphql is a function we call to execute the query, which is supplied as a string argument.

The `graphql` function returns a `Promise`. To simplify the code a bit, we use the `async`/`await` syntax instead. This allows us to have asynchronous code written in a synchronous style.

Once we have the slugs, we iterate over the results and call `createPage` for each. The `path` is the URL of the page, the `component` references our template page, and the `context` contains a `slug` property. This `slug` value is what is passed as an argument to the page query in our blog template page, which will be used to query for the full data for each blog post.

Linking to the dynamically generated pages

The last step in the process is to update our index page so that the blog post titles link to the full post pages that we dynamically created.

Open the file `src/components/BlogList.js`. In this component, we have a GraphQL query for the blog posts. We need to add the `slug` field to this query to get the URL of each blog post page, then we need to add links to those URLs.

Change the file to match the code in Listing 7-6.

Listing 7-6. The updated `BlogList` component

```
import React from 'react';

import { graphql, useStaticQuery } from 'gatsby';

import BlogPost from './BlogPost';

export default function BlogList() {
  const data = useStaticQuery(graphql`
    {
      allMarkdownRemark(sort: { fields: frontmatter___date, order: DESC })
      {
        edges {
          node {
            id
            frontmatter {
              title
```

```
            date(formatString: "MMMM D, YYYY")
          }
          fields {
            slug
          }
          excerpt
        }
      }
    }
  }
`);

  return (
    <div>
      {data.allMarkdownRemark.edges.map(edge => (
        <BlogPost
          key={edge.node.id}
          slug={edge.node.fields.slug}
          title={edge.node.frontmatter.title}
          date={edge.node.frontmatter.date}
          excerpt={edge.node.excerpt}
        />
      ))}
    </div>
  );
}
```

We are taking the slug from the query results and passing it as a prop to the `BlogPost` component, where it will render a link. Listing 7-7 shows the updated `BlogPost` component in `src/components/BlogPost.js`.

Listing 7-7. The updated `BlogPost` component

```
import React from 'react';

import { Link } from 'gatsby';
```

```
import styles from './BlogPost.module.css';

export default function BlogPost({ title, date, excerpt, slug }) {
  return (
    <article className={styles.blog}>
      <h2><Link to={slug}>{title}</Link></h2>
      <h3>{date}</h3>
      <p>{excerpt}</p>
    </article>
  );
}
```

The Gatsby `Link` component

Notice that we didn't add a standard HTML link via an anchor tag. Instead, we used Gatsby's built-in `Link` component. This is a special component meant to be used for navigation within a Gatsby site, which makes some optimizations and preloads some resources from the linked resources.

The optimization is very interesting. When the mouse is hovered over the link, it makes an asynchronous request for some metadata about the page being linked to.

If we open the browser's developer tools and monitor the network requests, we can see two requests are made when we hover over one of the links. One of these is `page-data.json`, which contains metadata specific to the page being linked to by that `Link` component. Listing 7-8 shows an example of a response from this call.

Listing 7-8. The contents of `page-data.json`

```
{
  "componentChunkName": "component---src-templates-blog-js",
  "path": "/2020-06-21-welcome-to-the-coffee-blog/",
  "result": {
    "data": {
      "markdownRemark": {
        "html": "...",
        "frontmatter": { "title": "Welcome to the Coffee Blog" }
      }
```

```
  },
  "pageContext": { "slug": "/2020-06-21-welcome-to-the-coffee-blog/" }
 }
}
```

This file contains a lot of information, including

- componentChunkName: The filename of the Webpack chunk containing this page

- path: The URL, relative to the site root

- result

  - data: The result of the GraphQL query that was executed at build time

  - pageContext: The data that was passed to the page component's context

We've made several changes. Let's see if everything is working. Save everything and run gatsby develop. Open the development site. The index page should now have links to each blog post, as shown in Figure 7-2.

Second Blog Post
June 26, 2020

This is the second blog post!

Welcome to the Coffee Blog
June 21, 2020

coffee cup Hello! Welcome to the Coffee Blog. This is our first blog post. Stay tuned for more information soon!

Figure 7-2. *The post titles are now links*

If we click one of the links, it should take us to a page for the full blog post. This is the page that we dynamically created using the Node APIs.

Figure 7-3. The full blog post page

One last tweak

Now that clicking a blog post title links us to the full blog post page, there is no way to get back to the index page (i.e., other than using the browser's back button). Let's make the header text a link back to the index page so that we have better navigation.

Open the file src/components/Layout.js, and add the code shown in Listing 7-9.

Listing 7-9. Adding a link to the index page

```
import React from 'react';

import { Link } from 'gatsby';
```

```
import styles from './Layout.module.css';

export default function Layout({ children }) {
  return (
    <div>
      <header id={styles.header}>
        <div id={styles.inner}>
          <h1><Link to="/">Joe's Coffee Shop</Link></h1>
        </div>
      </header>
      <main id={styles.main}>
        {children}
      </main>
    </div>
  );
}
```

This will result in a decidedly ugly link.

Figure 7-4. *The link has the default styling*

Let's make this look a little nicer. Open the CSS module in `src/components/Layout.module.css` and update it as shown in Listing 7-10.

Listing 7-10. The updated CSS module for the `Layout` component

```
#header {
  font-family: 'Oswald', sans-serif;
  background: url('/coffee.jpg');
  background-size: cover;
  color: #FFFFFF;
}
```

```
#header #inner {
  background: rgba(119, 79, 56, 0.85);
  padding: 1rem;
}

#header h1 {
  margin: 0;
}

#header h1 a {
  color: #FFFFFF;
  text-decoration: none;
}
```

The new header link is shown in Figure 7-5. It looks much better now.

Figure 7-5. *The restyled link*

Finally, to finish things up, let's commit and push to GitHub.

```
git add .
git commit -m "Add blog post pages"
git push origin master
```

Summary

In this chapter, we

- Created a template page to use for blog posts

- Used this template with Gatsby's Node APIs to dynamically create pages for blog posts

- Updated the index page to link to the blog posts

CHAPTER 8

Blog Pagination

Currently, we are displaying all of the blog posts on the index page. This is fine for just a handful of entries, but in most real-world sites, entries are broken up into pages. In this chapter, we will add some more blog entries and implement pagination.

How pagination works

We generate the list of blog posts by performing a GraphQL query. The query in its current form is shown in Listing 8-1.

Listing 8-1. The current GraphQL query

```
{
  allMarkdownRemark(sort: { fields: frontmatter___date, order: DESC }) {
    edges {
      node {
        id
        frontmatter {
          title
          date(formatString: "MMMM D, YYYY")
        }
        fields {
          slug
        }
        excerpt
      }
    }
  }
}
```

© Joe Attardi 2020
J. Attardi, *Using Gatsby and Netlify CMS*, https://doi.org/10.1007/978-1-4842-6297-9_8

The `allMarkdownRemark` field accepts several arguments. Currently, we're using the `sort` argument to define the sort order. There are several other arguments available as well. The two that are relevant to pagination are `skip` and `limit`. These define how many results to skip in the query results and how many results to return, respectively.

In order to do pagination in this way, we'll need to do some refactoring of the site. Currently, we are querying for blog entries in a static query in the `BlogList` component. In order to use the `skip` and `limit` arguments, we'll need to provide variables to the query. However, static queries can't use variables - only page queries can. This means we need to use a page component for the blog list.

We'll create a new blog page template that will list a given page of blog posts. Then, using Gatsby's `createPages` API, we'll query for the total number of blog posts, divide that into pages, then dynamically create a `blog/<page number>` page for each page of posts. For each page we create, we'll pass some context parameters that will be used as variables in the page's GraphQL query, filling in values for the `skip` and `limit` arguments.

Finally, we'll update the index page so that it shows the first three posts, with a link to the full paginated list at the bottom.

Creating some new blog entries

Before we can use pagination, we need enough blog posts to necessitate pagination. Log in to the CMS at https://<your-site-name>.netlify.app/admin, and add some new blog posts. If you aren't feeling particularly creative, you can go to `https://lipsum.com` to generate some "Lorem Ipsum" placeholder text. We will use a page size of 5, and we want to have more than one page of posts, so go ahead and create six to ten blog posts.

Hopefully that wasn't too tedious. Remember that each new blog post creates a new commit in the Git repository, so pull the latest code from GitHub before proceeding.

Dynamically creating the blog list pages

The first page of the blog list will be at the path /blog. Subsequent pages will have a page number added to them: /blog/2, /blog/3, etc. Open the file `gatsby-node.js`, and add the code shown in Listing 8-2. This code is based on code from the Gatsby documentation, which can be found at `www.gatsbyjs.org/docs/adding-pagination/`.

Listing 8-2. The updated gatsby-node.js file

```
const path = require('path');

const { createFilePath } = require('gatsby-source-filesystem');

exports.onCreateNode = function({ node, getNode, actions }) {
  const { createNodeField } = actions;

  if (node.internal.type === 'MarkdownRemark') {
    const slug = createFilePath({ node, getNode });
    createNodeField({
      node,
      name: 'slug',
      value: slug
    });
  }
};

exports.createPages = async function({ graphql, actions }) {
  const { createPage } = actions;

  const result = await graphql(`
    query {
      allMarkdownRemark {
        edges {
          node {
            fields {
              slug
            }
          }
        }
      }
    }
  `);
```

```
  result.data.allMarkdownRemark.edges
    .forEach(({ node }) => {
      createPage({
        path: node.fields.slug,
        component: path
          .resolve('./src/templates/blog.js'),
        context: {
          slug: node.fields.slug
        }
      });
    });

    const posts = result.data.allMarkdownRemark.edges;
    const pageSize = 5;
    const pageCount = Math.ceil(posts.length / pageSize);

    const templatePath = path.resolve('src/templates/blog-list.js');

    for (let i = 0; i < pageCount; i++) {
      let path = '/blog';
      if (i > 0) {
        path += `/${i + 1}`;
      }

      createPage({
        path,
        component: templatePath,
        context: {
          limit: pageSize,
          skip: i * pageSize,
          pageCount,
          currentPage: i + 1
        }
      });
    }
};
```

First, we calculate the number of pages based on the page size and total number of posts. We then loop through each page number, dynamically creating a page for each, using the `blog-list.js` template page.

When creating each page, we pass some context data to it:

- `limit`: The value to use for the limit argument. This is just the number of posts per page, so it will be the same for each page.

- `skip`: The value to use for the skip argument. This will ensure that the query skips the posts from all previous pages and starts at the right one.

- `pageCount`: The total number of pages. This is passed to each page so the page can determine if it is the last page or not, as we don't want to show a "next page" link on the last page.

- `currentPage`: The current page. This is used to determine if a page is the first page, where it shouldn't show a "previous page" link, or the last page, where it shouldn't show a "next page" link.

Creating the blog list template page

Now we'll create the template page. Create a new file `src/templates/blog-list.js` and add the code from Listing 8-3. This code is adapted from "Pagination in GatsbyJS" by Nicky Meuleman. The original code can be found at `https://nickymeuleman.netlify.app/blog/gatsby-pagination`.

Listing 8-3. The blog list template page

```
import React from 'react';

import { graphql, Link } from 'gatsby';

import BlogPost from '../components/BlogPost';
import Layout from '../components/Layout';

import styles from './blog-list.module.css';


export default function BlogListTemplate({ data, pageContext }) {
  // Generate the previous and next page URLs.
```

```
const previousPage = pageContext.currentPage === 2 ?
  '/blog' :
  `/blog/${pageContext.currentPage - 1}`;
const nextPage = `/blog/${pageContext.currentPage + 1}`;

return (
  <Layout>
    <div id={styles.hero}>
      <h1>The Coffee Blog</h1>
    </div>
    <main className={styles.blogList}>
      {data.allMarkdownRemark.edges.map(node => (
        <BlogPost
          key={node.node.id}
          slug={node.node.fields.slug}
          title={node.node.frontmatter.title}
          date={node.node.frontmatter.date}
          excerpt={node.node.excerpt} />
      ))}
    </main>

    <div id={styles.pageLinks}>
      {pageContext.currentPage > 1 && (
        <Link to={previousPage}>
          << Previous Page
        </Link>
      )}

      {pageContext.currentPage < pageContext.pageCount && (
        <Link to={nextPage}>
          Next Page >>
        </Link>
      )}
    </div>
  </Layout>
)
}
```

```
// The page query.
export const query = graphql`
  query BlogListQuery($skip: Int!, $limit: Int!) {
    allMarkdownRemark(
      sort: { fields: [frontmatter___date], order: DESC }
      filter: { frontmatter: { contentKey: { eq: "blog" }}}
      limit: $limit
      skip: $skip
    ) {
      edges {
        node {
          id
          frontmatter {
            title
            date(formatString: "MMMM D, YYYY")
          }
          fields {
            slug
          }
          excerpt
        }
      }
    }
  }
`;
```

The BlogListTemplate component takes two props:

- data: The result of the GraphQL query

- pageContext: The page context data we passed to the createPage function

First, we generate the URLs to the previous and next pages. We then iterate over the query results and render a BlogPost component for each blog post in the results, passing in all the required props.

After rendering the list of posts, we render the previous page (if we aren't on the first page) and next page (if we aren't on the last page) links.

Lastly, we add the page query. This query is very similar to the query we used in the
BlogList component. The main difference is that we specify limit and skip arguments
for pagination. These will be substituted for the values of limit and skip from the page
context before running the query.

Let's also create the CSS module for the blog list template page. Create a new file
src/templates/blog-list.module.css, as shown in Listing 8-4.

Listing 8-4. The CSS module for the blog list

```css
#hero {
  background: url('/latte.jpg');
  background-size: cover;
  height: 25rem;
  display: flex;
  flex-direction: column;
  align-items: center;
  justify-content: center;
}

#hero h1 {
  margin: 0;
  text-transform: uppercase;
  font-size: 5rem;
  padding: 0.5rem;
  border-radius: 5px;
  background: rgba(255, 255, 255, 0.5);
}

.blog-list {
  padding: 1rem;
}

#page-links {
  padding: 1rem;
}

#page-links a {
  margin: 1rem;
}
```

Now, let's restart the local server by running `gatsby develop`. Go to the URL http://localhost:8000/blog. You should see the first five blog posts with a "Next Page" link at the bottom of the page as seen in Figure 8-1.

Figure 8-1. *The first page of blog posts*

Clicking the "Next Page" link should go to the next page of blog posts, which will have a "Previous Page" link.

Adding a link to the new blog list page

Let's add a link in the site header to the new blog list page. Because it is a link to another page on the site, we will use the Gatsby Link component. Open the file src/components/Layout.js and update it with the code in Listing 8-5.

Listing 8-5. Adding a link to the header

```
import React from 'react';

import { Link } from 'gatsby';

import styles from './Layout.module.css';

export default function Layout({ children }) {
  return (
    <div>
      <header id={styles.header}>
        <div id={styles.inner}>
          <h1><Link to="/">Joe's Coffee Shop</Link></h1>
          <Link to="/blog">Blog</Link>
        </div>
      </header>
      <main id={styles.main}>
        {children}
      </main>
    </div>
  );
}
```

Next, open the CSS module src/components/Layout.module.css and update it with the code in Listing 8-6.

Listing 8-6. The updated CSS module

```
#header {
  font-family: 'Oswald', sans-serif;
  background: url('/coffee.jpg');
  background-size: cover;
  color: #FFFFFF;
}

#header #inner {
  background: rgba(119, 79, 56, 0.85);
  padding: 1rem;
  display: flex;
  align-items: center;
}

#header h1 {
  margin: 0;
  flex-grow: 1;
}

#header h1 a {
  color: #FFFFFF;
  text-decoration: none;
}

#header a {
  color: #FFFFFF;
  text-decoration: none;
}
```

Refresh the page, and now there should be a link in the site header that goes to the blog list page, as shown in Figure 8-2.

Figure 8-2. The blog link in the header

Updating the index page

Currently, the index page shows all the blog posts. This will make the index page very long over time as more blog posts are added (and defeats the purpose of the separate blog list page).

We can update the GraphQL query in the BlogList component used on the index page to just show the first three posts, then have a link to the full blog list at the end.

Open the file src/components/BlogList.js, and make the changes shown in Listing 8-7.

Listing 8-7. Limiting the number of blog posts in the BlogList component

```
import React from 'react';

import { Link, graphql, useStaticQuery } from 'gatsby';

import BlogPost from './BlogPost';

export default function BlogList() {
  const data = useStaticQuery(graphql`
    {
      allMarkdownRemark(
        sort: { fields: frontmatter___date, order: DESC }
        limit: 3
        ) {
        edges {
          node {
            id
            frontmatter {
              title
              date(formatString: "MMMM D, YYYY")
            }
            fields {
              slug
            }
            excerpt
          }
        }
```

```
      }
    }
  `);

  return (
    <div>
      {data.allMarkdownRemark.edges.map(edge => (
        <BlogPost
          key={edge.node.id}
          slug={edge.node.fields.slug}
          title={edge.node.frontmatter.title}
          date={edge.node.frontmatter.date}
          excerpt={edge.node.excerpt}
        />
      ))}
      <div>
        <Link to="/blog">More >></Link>
      </div>
    </div>
  );
}
```

If we refresh the site now, the index page should only be showing three blog posts, followed by a link to the full blog list page.

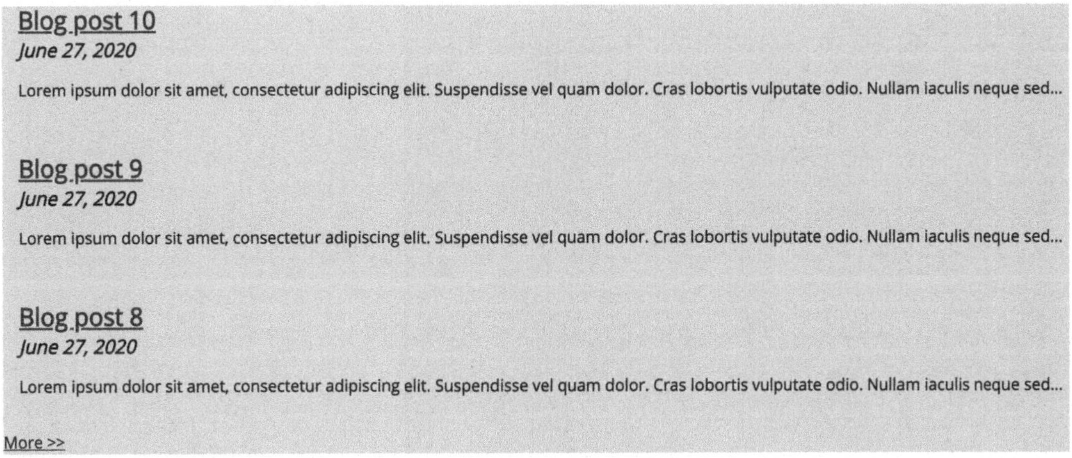

Blog post 10
June 27, 2020

Lorem ipsum dolor sit amet, consectetur adipiscing elit. Suspendisse vel quam dolor. Cras lobortis vulputate odio. Nullam iaculis neque sed...

Blog post 9
June 27, 2020

Lorem ipsum dolor sit amet, consectetur adipiscing elit. Suspendisse vel quam dolor. Cras lobortis vulputate odio. Nullam iaculis neque sed...

Blog post 8
June 27, 2020

Lorem ipsum dolor sit amet, consectetur adipiscing elit. Suspendisse vel quam dolor. Cras lobortis vulputate odio. Nullam iaculis neque sed...

More >>

Figure 8-3. *Only three blog posts on the index page*

Now that we have added blog post pagination, let's create a new commit and push our code:

```
git add .
git commit -m "Add blog pagination"
git push origin master
```

Summary

In this chapter, we

- Learned about the `skip` and `limit` arguments to a GraphQL query, which are used for pagination

- Dynamically created blog list pages so they aren't all shown on a single page

- Used context data passed to the template page to conditionally render previous page and next page links

- Added a link to the new blog list page from the index page

CHAPTER 9

Adding More Content

The index page currently has a hard-coded hero image and tagline, as shown in Figure 9-1.

Figure 9-1. *The current index page*

In this chapter, we'll make this content configurable through the CMS application.

© Joe Attardi 2020
J. Attardi, *Using Gatsby and Netlify CMS*, https://doi.org/10.1007/978-1-4842-6297-9_9

The contentKey field

As we've seen earlier, Netlify CMS stores all its data in Markdown files. We will configure some new content for the index page that will be stored in a Markdown file. There's a slight problem, however. In gatsby-node.js we are querying for all the Markdown files to generate blog pages. This means it will generate a new page for every Markdown file. This is a problem, because we don't want a blog page to be generated for Markdown files containing page data. We need some way to distinguish blog entries from other data.

To do this, we'll introduce a new field to all of our collections called contentKey. We'll use this field to identify the content type of Markdown files, to distinguish blog posts from other types of content. We can do this with a hidden field in the CMS configuration.

A hidden field does not appear in the CMS user interface. Its value exists only in the Markdown file. The value of this field for a given collection is set with the default property of the field.

To get started, open the CMS configuration file static/admin/config.yml. This is where we configured the blog collection. Let's add the hidden contentKey field to the blog collection, as shown in Listing 9-1.

Listing 9-1. The updated CMS configuration file

```
backend:
  name: git-gateway
  branch: master

media_folder: static/img
public_folder: /img

collections:
  - name: "blog"
    label: "Blog"
    folder: "src/blog"
    create: true
    slug: "{{year}}-{{month}}-{{day}}-{{slug}}"
    fields:
      - name: "contentKey"
        widget: "hidden"
```

```
      default: "blog"
    - label: "Title"
      name: "title"
      widget: "string"
    - label: "Publish Date"
      name: "date"
      widget: "datetime"
    - label: "Body"
      name: "body"
      widget: "markdown"
```

Now that we've added the contentKey field, it will be added to each new blog post we create. Unfortunately, it won't update existing blog entries. We'll have to do that ourselves. Open the src/blog folder, and in each Markdown file, add contentKey: blog to the front matter, like the example shown in Listing 9-2.

Listing 9-2. Adding the contentKey field to the front matter

```
---
title: Second Blog Post
date: 2020-06-26T20:00:48.463Z
contentKey: blog
---
This is the second blog post!
```

Now that we've tagged all of our blog posts with a contentKey of blog, we'll need to make a slight change to gatsby-node.js so that it only creates blog post pages for Markdown files that are actually blog posts.

Open gatsby-node.js and update the createPages function as shown in Listing 9-3.

Listing 9-3. Conditional page creation

```
const path = require('path');

const { createFilePath } = require('gatsby-source-filesystem');

exports.onCreateNode = function({ node, getNode, actions }) {
  const { createNodeField } = actions;
```

115

```
  if (node.internal.type === 'MarkdownRemark') {
    const slug = createFilePath({ node, getNode });
    createNodeField({
      node,
      name: 'slug',
      value: slug
    });
  }
};

exports.createPages = async function({ graphql, actions }) {
  const { createPage } = actions;

  const result = await graphql(`
    query {
      allMarkdownRemark {
        edges {
          node {
            frontmatter {
              contentKey
            }
            fields {
              slug
            }
          }
        }
      }
    }
  `);

  const posts = result.data.allMarkdownRemark.edges
    .filter(edge => edge.node.frontmatter.contentKey === 'blog');
  posts
    .forEach(({ node }) => {
      createPage({
        path: node.fields.slug,
        component: path
```

```
      .resolve('./src/templates/blog.js'),
    context: {
      slug: node.fields.slug
    }
  });
});

const pageSize = 5;
const pageCount = Math.ceil(posts.length / pageSize);

const templatePath = path.resolve('src/templates/blog-list.js');

for (let i = 0; i < pageCount; i++) {
  let path = '/blog';
  if (i > 0) {
    path += `/${i + 1}`;
  };

  createPage({
    path,
    component: templatePath,
    context: {
      limit: pageSize,
      skip: i * pageSize,
      pageCount,
      currentPage: i + 1
    }
  });
}
};
```

We've made a few changes here to the createPages function. First, we add the contentKey from the front matter to the GraphQL query. Then, we filter the list of returned Markdown nodes so that we only create pages for nodes whose contentKey is blog.

There's one other change we need to make. We need to modify the GraphQL query in the blog list template page so that it only queries for nodes with a contentKey of blog. Open the file src/templates/blog-list.js and make the changes indicated in Listing 9-4.

Listing 9-4. Modifying the GraphQL query

```
import React from 'react';

import { graphql, Link } from 'gatsby';

import BlogPost from '../components/BlogPost';
import Layout from '../components/Layout';

import styles from './blog-list.module.css';

export default function BlogListTemplate({ data, pageContext }) {
  // Generate the previous and next page URLs.
  const previousPage = pageContext.currentPage === 2 ?
    '/blog' :
    `/blog/${pageContext.currentPage - 1}`;
  const nextPage = `/blog/${pageContext.currentPage + 1}`;

  return (
    <Layout>
      <div id={styles.hero}>
        <h1>The Coffee Blog</h1>
      </div>
      <main className={styles.blogList}>
        {data.allMarkdownRemark.edges.map(node => (
          <BlogPost
            key={node.node.id}
            slug={node.node.fields.slug}
            title={node.node.frontmatter.title}
            date={node.node.frontmatter.date}
            excerpt={node.node.excerpt} />
        ))}
      </main>

      <div id={styles.pageLinks}>
      {pageContext.currentPage > 1 && (
          <Link to={previousPage}>
            << Previous Page
          </Link>
```

```
      )}

        {pageContext.currentPage < pageContext.pageCount && (
          <Link to={nextPage}>
            Next Page >>
          </Link>
        )}
      </div>
    </Layout>
  )
}

// The page query.
export const query = graphql`
  query BlogListQuery($skip: Int!, $limit: Int!) {
    allMarkdownRemark(
      sort: { fields: [frontmatter___date], order: DESC }
      filter: { frontmatter: { contentKey: { eq: "blog" }}}
      limit: $limit
      skip: $skip
    ) {
      edges {
        node {
          id
          frontmatter {
            title
            date(formatString: "MMMM D, YYYY")
          }
          fields {
            slug
          }
          excerpt
        }
      }
    }
  }
`;
```

We'll also need to change the GraphQL query in the BlogList component that's used on the index page. Open the file src/components/BlogList.js, and make the change indicated in Listing 9-5.

Listing 9-5. Modifying the GraphQL query in the BlogList component

```
import React from 'react';

import { Link, graphql, useStaticQuery } from 'gatsby';

import BlogPost from './BlogPost';

export default function BlogList() {
  const data = useStaticQuery(graphql`
    {
      allMarkdownRemark(
        sort: { fields: frontmatter___date, order: DESC }
        filter: { frontmatter: { contentKey: { eq: "blog" }}}
        limit: 3
        ) {
        edges {
          node {
            id
            frontmatter {
              title
              date(formatString: "MMMM D, YYYY")
            }
            fields {
              slug
            }
            excerpt
          }
        }
      }
    }
  `);
```

```
  return (
    <div>
      {data.allMarkdownRemark.edges.map(edge => (
        <BlogPost
          key={edge.node.id}
          slug={edge.node.fields.slug}
          title={edge.node.frontmatter.title}
          date={edge.node.frontmatter.date}
          excerpt={edge.node.excerpt}
        />
      ))}
      <div>
        <Link to="/blog">More >></Link>
      </div>
    </div>
  );
}
```

Since we changed gatsby-node.js, we have to restart the development server. When we rerun gatsby develop, then go to http://localhost:8000/blog, we should see the same blog post listing as before.

Let's stop here and make a commit:

```
git add .
git commit -m "Add `blog` contentKey"
git push origin master
```

Creating a pages collection

Our existing blog collection is a folder collection. To store the data about our index page, and other content, we'll create a file collection called pages. Each element of this collection will correspond to a different page of the site. We'll start this collection with the index page.

Open the CMS configuration file, static/admin/config.yml, and add the new pages collection as shown in Listing 9-6.

Listing 9-6. Adding the pages collection

```
backend:
  name: git-gateway
  branch: master

media_folder: static/img
public_folder: /img

collections:
  - name: "blog"
    label: "Blog"
    folder: "src/blog"
    create: true
    slug: "{{year}}-{{month}}-{{day}}-{{slug}}"
    fields:
      - name: "contentKey"
        widget: "hidden"
        default: "blog"
      - label: "Title"
        name: "title"
        widget: "string"
      - label: "Publish Date"
        name: "date"
        widget: "datetime"
      - label: "Body"
        name: "body"
        widget: "markdown"
  - name: "pages"
    label: "Pages"
    files:
      - file: "src/pageData/index.md"
        label: "Index Page"
        name: "index-page"
        fields:
          - name: "contentKey"
            widget: "hidden"
```

```
        default: "indexPage"
      - label: "Tagline"
        name: "tagline"
        widget: "string"
      - label: "Hero Image"
        name: "heroImage"
        widget: "image"
```

We have added a new collection, called `pages`, which will contain the page data. The index page has a `contentKey` of `indexPage` and includes a `tagline` and `heroImage` field.

Before proceeding, we will need to create the `src/pageData` directory and add a skeleton `index.md` file. Add the skeleton front matter, including the `contentKey`, shown in Listing 9-7.

Listing 9-7. Adding the index page data

```
---
contentKey: indexPage
---
```

After making these changes, let's commit and push the changes.

```
git add .
git commit -m "Add pages collection"
git push origin master
```

Adding the index page data

Once Netlify deploys the new version of the site, log in to the CMS application. You'll see a new collection called "Pages." Under "Pages," there should be one entry – the Index page.

Figure 9-2. *The new Pages collection*

Click on "Index Page," and you will see a text widget and an image widget, just as we configured in the configuration file.

Figure 9-3. *The fields for the index page*

Before filling this in, we'll need a suitable large image. A good source for free images is Unsplash (`https://unsplash.com`). Once you have downloaded an image to use, go back to the CMS, and edit the Index page.

Enter a value for "Tagline," then under "Hero Image," click "Choose an image." The media manager will appear. From here, click the "Upload" button, and select the image you downloaded. The image will be uploaded and will appear in "Draft" status. Click "Choose selected" to select the image.

Figure 9-4. *The media manager*

Once you have entered a value for the tagline and selected a hero image, go to the top right and click "Publish," then "Publish now".

Go to the terminal and perform a git pull operation:

```
git pull origin master
```

A new commit will be downloaded from GitHub. If you check the file src/pageData/index.md, you will see it now contains the tagline and hero image you specified in the CMS.

Adding another filesystem source

Currently, the gatsby-source-filesystem plugin is only sourcing content from the src/blog directory. Before we can query the page data, we'll need to add a new instance of the plugin that gets file content from the src/pageData directory. Open the gatsby-config.js file, and add the new instance to the plugins section, as shown in Listing 9-8.

Listing 9-8. The updated configuration file

```
module.exports = {
  siteMetadata: {
    title: 'The Coffee Blog'
  },

  plugins: [
    'gatsby-plugin-netlify-cms',
    {
      resolve: 'gatsby-source-filesystem',
      options: {
        name: 'blog',
        path: 'src/blog'
      }
    },
    {
      resolve: 'gatsby-source-filesystem',
      options: {
        name: 'pageData',
        path: 'src/pageData'
      }
    },
    'gatsby-transformer-remark'
  ]
};
```

Using the CMS content in the index page

Now that we've defined the content for the index page in the CMS, let's update the index page to use it. Open the file src/pages/index.js and make the changes indicated in Listing 9-9.

Listing 9-9. Adding CMS content to the GraphQL query

```
import React from 'react';

import { graphql, useStaticQuery } from 'gatsby';
```

```
import BlogList from '../components/BlogList';
import Layout from '../components/Layout';

import styles from './index.module.css';

export default function IndexPage() {
  const data = useStaticQuery(graphql`
    {
      site {
        siteMetadata {
          title
        }
      }
      markdownRemark(frontmatter: { contentKey: { eq: "indexPage" } }) {
        frontmatter {
          tagline
          heroImage
        }
      }
    }
  `);

  const tagline = data.markdownRemark.frontmatter.tagline;
  const heroImage = data.markdownRemark.frontmatter.heroImage;

  return (
    <Layout>
      <div
        id={styles.hero}
        style={{ backgroundImage: `url('${heroImage}')` }}>
        <h1>{tagline}</h1>
      </div>
      <BlogList />
    </Layout>
  );
}
```

We add the markdownRemark field to the GraphQL query, looking up the Markdown file with a contentKey of indexPage. We then query for the tagline and heroImage fields in the front matter.

Next, we extract the tagline and hero image URL from the query results and utilize them in the page component.

Since we made plugin changes, we'll need to restart the Gatsby development server. Once you have restarted the server, go to the index page at http://localhost:8000, and you should see the tagline and hero image that we configured in the CMS as shown in Figure 9-5.

Figure 9-5. *The new index page, containing the CMS data*

That's it. Later, we can change the tagline or hero image by just editing them in the CMS application – no code changes are required. This is the real power of Netlify CMS.

Let's finish this chapter by committing and pushing to GitHub:

```
git add .
git commit -m "Use CMS data in index page"
git push origin master
```

Summary

In this chapter, we

- Created a new pages file collection in the CMS for individual page data

- Created a file to store the index page data

- Updated the index page to make a GraphQL query for the CMS data and display it

CHAPTER 10

Creating the Coffee Menu

What good is a coffee shop without a menu? In this chapter we will add a menu to our coffee shop site. The contents of the menu will be managed through Netlify CMS. The menu will have different categories containing different drinks and bakery items, with descriptions and prices.

Nested lists

One of the many widget types in Netlify CMS is the List widget. A List contains other widgets, or sets of widgets, and items can be added and removed in the Content Manager. Lists can even contain other lists.

We'll use the List widget type in our menu. The menu will consist of a list of categories – for example, Hot Drinks, Iced Drinks, or Bakery. Each category will, in turn, contain a list of menu items.

Defining the menu page

For the menu, we'll add a new page under the Pages collection. Right now, this collection contains one page – the index page. Let's add the menu page and its fields. Open the file `static/admin/config.yml` and update it with the code in Listing 10-1.

Listing 10-1. Adding the Menu page to the configuration file

```
backend:
  name: git-gateway
  branch: master

media_folder: static/img
public_folder: /img
```

© Joe Attardi 2020
J. Attardi, *Using Gatsby and Netlify CMS*, https://doi.org/10.1007/978-1-4842-6297-9_10

```
collections:
  - name: "blog"
    label: "Blog"
    folder: "src/blog"
    create: true
    slug: "{{year}}-{{month}}-{{day}}-{{slug}}"
    fields:
      - name: "contentKey"
        widget: "hidden"
        default: "blog"
      - label: "Title"
        name: "title"
        widget: "string"
      - label: "Publish Date"
        name: "date"
        widget: "datetime"
      - label: "Body"
        name: "body"
        widget: "markdown"
  - name: "pages"
    label: "Pages"
    files:
      - file: "src/pageData/index.md"
        label: "Index Page"
        name: "index-page"
        fields:
          - name: "contentKey"
            widget: "hidden"
            default: "indexPage"
          - label: "Tagline"
            name: "tagline"
            widget: "string"
          - label: "Hero Image"
            name: "heroImage"
            widget: "image"
```

```
- file: "src/pageData/menu.md"
  label: "Menu"
  name: "menu"
  fields:
    - name: "contentKey"
      widget: "hidden"
      default: "menu"
    - label: "Title"
      name: "title"
      widget: "string"
    - label: "Categories"
      label_singular: "Category"
      name: "categories"
      widget: "list"
      fields:
        - label: "Name"
          name: "name"
          widget: "string"
        - label: "Items"
          label_singular: "Item"
          name: "items"
          widget: "list"
          fields:
            - label: "Name"
              name: "name"
              widget: "string"
            - label: "Description"
              name: "description"
              widget: "text"
            - label: "Price"
              name: "price"
              widget: "string"
```

The Menu page has a list of categories, which in turn each contain a list of items.

You might notice we are using the `label_singular` property in a few places. When viewing the Menu page in the CMS, it will list "Categories" and "Items." Without the `label_singular` property, the add buttons would be labeled "Add Categories" and "Add Items." `label_singular` is used for the label on those buttons so that they are grammatically correct: "Add Category" and "Add Item."

Once you have made the indicated changes, make a commit and push to GitHub:

```
git add .
git commit -m "Add menu page"
git push origin master
```

Adding menu items

Once Netlify has deployed the new version of the site, open the CMS application. On the Home page, you should now see the Menu page listed after the index page in the "Pages" collection, as shown in Figure 10-1.

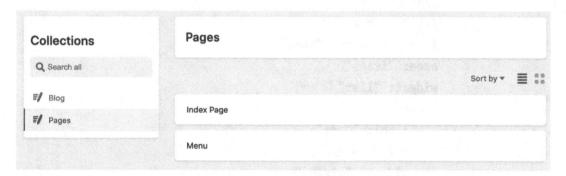

Figure 10-1. *The new Menu page shown in the CMS*

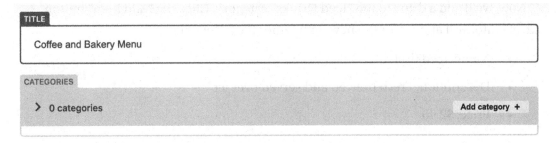

Figure 10-2. *The title and empty category list*

Click the "Menu" page. For the "Title" field, enter "Coffee and Bakery Menu." Below the title, you will see a UI for adding new menu categories.

Let's add our first category, Iced Drinks. Click the "Add category" button, and a new editor will appear for adding the new category. Enter "Iced Drinks" in the "Name" field. Just like with the category list, there is now an empty list for the menu items in the new category.

TITLE

Coffee and Bakery Menu

CATEGORIES

⌄ 1 category   Add category +

⌄   =   ✕

NAME

Iced Drinks

ITEMS

> 0 items   Add item +

Figure 10-3. *Adding a new category*

Now, we'll add a drink to the "Iced Drinks" category. Click the "Add item" button, and an editor will appear for the new item. Enter the following:

- Name: Iced Coffee

- Description: Fresh brewed and served over ice

- Price: $2.49

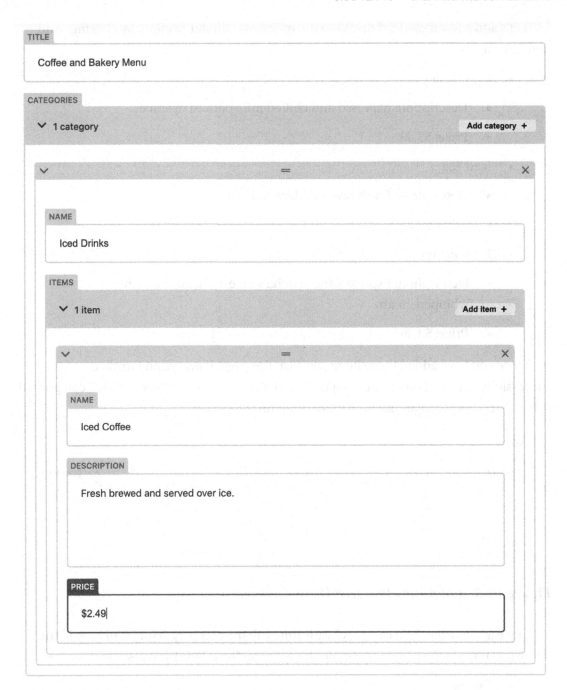

Figure 10-4. *Adding the first menu item*

Let's add a few more iced drinks to the menu in a similar fashion, by clicking "Add item" again.

- Iced Latte
  - Description: Espresso and chilled milk poured over ice
  - Price: $3.49
- Iced Tea
  - Description: Fresh brewed black tea leaves
  - Price: $2.25
- Iced Mocha
  - Description: Espresso and mocha sauce, milk and ice, with whipped cream
  - Price: $3.49

Once you have added these items, publish the page. If everything worked successfully, let's add one more category. Click the caret for the "Iced Drinks" category to collapse it. This just gives us some more room on the screen.

Figure 10-5. *Collapsing the "Iced Drinks" category*

Once again, click "Add category." This time call the category "Hot Drinks." Add the following items in the same way as you did with the "Iced Drinks" category:

- Coffee
  - Description: Fresh brewed Colombian coffee
  - Price: $1.99

- Cappuccino

    - Description: Espresso with frothed milk

    - Price: $2.49

- Hot Cocoa

    - Description: Steamed milk with chocolate syrup

    - Price: $1.49

Once again, click "Publish" then "Publish now" in the upper right corner.

Next, open a terminal and go to the project directory. Perform a `git pull` operation:

```
git pull origin master
```

You should get two new commits, containing the new menu data we just added from the CMS, in the file `src/pageData/menu.md`.

Building the menu page

Before we create the menu page, let's add a link in the header to the menu. Open the file `src/components/Layout.js,` and add a `Link` to `/menu`, as shown in Listing 10-2.

Listing 10-2. Adding a link to the menu page

```
import React from 'react';

import { Link } from 'gatsby';

import styles from './Layout.module.css';

export default function Layout({ children }) {
  return (
    <div>
      <header id={styles.header}>
        <div id={styles.inner}>
          <h1><Link to="/">Joe's Coffee Shop</Link></h1>
          <Link to="/blog">Blog</Link>
          <Link to="/menu">Menu</Link>
        </div>
```

```
    </header>
    <main id={styles.main}>
      {children}
    </main>
  </div>
);
}
```

Start the development server by running gatsby develop and go to the index page. The links don't look quite right in the header – there's no whitespace between them.

Figure 10-6. *The header links*

We can fix this with a slight tweak to the layout's CSS module. Open the file src/ components/Layout.module.css and add a slight margin between links, as shown in Listing 10-3.

Listing 10-3. Adding margin to the links

```
#header {
  font-family: 'Oswald', sans-serif;
  background: url('/coffee.jpg');
  background-size: cover;
  color: #FFFFFF;
}

#header #inner {
  background: rgba(119, 79, 56, 0.85);
  padding: 1rem;
  display: flex;
  align-items: center;
}

#header h1 {
```

```
  margin: 0;
  flex-grow: 1;
}

#header h1 a {
  color: #FFFFFF;
  text-decoration: none;
}

#header a {
  color: #FFFFFF;
  text-decoration: none;
  margin: 0.5rem;
}
```

Figure 10-7. *Better spacing between links*

The links have some space between them now. Next, we need to create the page for the menu. First, let's create a reusable `MenuCategory` component that we'll use on the menu page. Create a new file `src/components/MenuCategory.js,` and add the code from Listing 10-4.

Listing 10-4. The `MenuCategory` component

```
import React from 'react';

import styles from './MenuCategory.module.css';

export default function MenuCategory({ category }) {
  return (
    <div className={styles.category}>
      <h2>{category.name}</h2>
      <ul>
        {category.items.map(item => (
```

```
      <li key={item.name}>
        <div className={styles.name}>{item.name}</div>
        <div className={styles.description}>{item.description}</div>
        <div>{item.price}</div>
      </li>
    ))}
  </ul>
</div>
);
}
```

This is a simple presentational component. A menu category is passed as a prop, and the category's items are rendered in order. Next, let's create the CSS module referenced in this file. Create the file src/components/MenuCategory.module.css, and add the code from Listing 10-5.

Listing 10-5. Styles for the MenuCategory component

```css
.category {
  margin: 1rem 2rem;
  width: 15rem;
}

.category h2 {
  margin: 0;
  margin-bottom: 1px solid #774f38;
}

.category ul {
  padding: 0;
}

.category li {
  list-style-type: none;
  display: flex;
  flex-direction: column;
  margin: 1rem;
}
```

```css
.name {
  font-weight: bold;
  font-size: 1.2rem;
}

.description {
  font-style: italic;
}
```

Now that we've created the `MenuCategory` component, let's go back and create the menu page. Create the file `src/pages/menu.js` and add the code from Listing 10-6.

Listing 10-6. The menu page

```javascript
import React from 'react';

import Layout from '../components/Layout';
import MenuCategory from '../components/MenuCategory';

import { graphql, useStaticQuery } from 'gatsby';

import styles from './menu.module.css';

export default function Menu() {
  const data = useStaticQuery(graphql`
    {
      markdownRemark(frontmatter: { contentKey: { eq: "menu" } }) {
        frontmatter {
          title
          categories {
            name
            items {
              name
              description
              price
            }
          }
        }
```

```
      }
    }
  `);

  return (
    <Layout>
      <div id={styles.main}>
        <h1>{data.markdownRemark.frontmatter.title}</h1>
        <div id={styles.menu}>
          {data.markdownRemark.frontmatter.categories.map(category => (
            <MenuCategory
              key={category.name}
              category={category} />
          ))}
        </div>
      </div>
    </Layout>
  );
}
```

Next, let's create the CSS module. Create the file src/pages/menu.module.css and add the code in Listing 10-7.

Listing 10-7. The styles for the menu page

```css
#main {
  padding: 1rem;
}

#main h1 {
  margin: 0;
}

#menu {
  display: flex;
}
```

There's one last step needed. When we created the menu page data, the CMS created the Markdown file containing the menu data. However, it did not add the contentKey field to the front matter. We'll need to add that manually as a one-time step.

Open the file src/pageData/menu.md. Add the contentKey field as shown in
Listing 10-8.

Listing 10-8. Adding the contentKey to the menu page data

```
---
title: Coffee and Bakery Menu
contentKey: menu
categories:
  - name: Iced Drinks
    items:
      - name: Iced Coffee
        description: Fresh brewed and served over ice.
        price: "$2.49 "
      - name: Iced Latte
        description: Espresso and chilled milk poured over ice.
        price: $3.49
      - name: Iced Tea
        description: Fresh brewed black tea leaves.
        price: $2.25
      - name: Iced Mocha
        description: Espresso and mocha sauce, milk and ice, with whipped
cream.
        price: $3.49
  - name: Hot Drinks
    items:
      - name: Coffee
        description: Fresh brewed Colombian coffee.
        price: $1.99
      - name: Cappuccino
        description: Espresso with frothed milk.
        price: $2.49
      - name: Hot Cocoa
        description: Steamed milk with chocolate syrup.
        price: $1.49
---
```

Once this is done, restart the development server, and navigate to http://localhost:8000/menu. The menu page should be shown, including all the menu items we added.

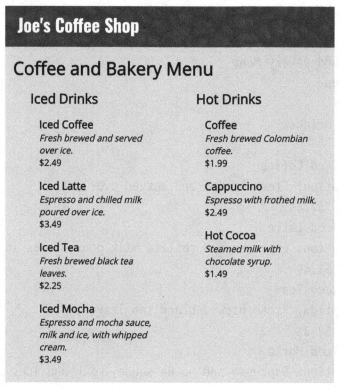

Figure 10-8. *The menu page*

Lastly, as always, let's commit and push:

```
git add .
git commit -m "Add coffee menu"
git push origin master
```

Ease of maintenance

We've created a fully customizable coffee and bakery menu. Now, the managers of the coffee shop can add items or adjust prices, all without writing a single line of code. Later, we'll add a custom preview component so that they can see a live preview of what the rendered menu page will look like.

Summary

In this chapter, we

- Added a new page to the CMS for the menu

- Added some menu categories and items

- Created a menu page to query the menu data with GraphQL and display it

CHAPTER 11

Working with Images

In Chapter 9, we added a hero image to the index page. If you got the image from Unsplash, as recommended, you might notice that the image file is very large. This could result in slow loading times for some users of the site.

Gatsby has plugins that work with an image processing library called Sharp (`https://sharp.pixelplumbing.com/`) to resize and crop images in various ways at build time. This can be combined with the `gatsby-image` plugin to create a powerful image processing pipeline.

Using these plugins also provides two effects to show "placeholder" images as the full image is loading:

- Blur-up: Creates an extremely small size of the image that will load very quickly and sets that as the image, blurred, while the full image loads

- Traced placeholder: Creates an SVG showing the outline of the full image that is displayed while the full image loads

In this chapter, we'll use these plugins to optimize the hero image on the index page.

Plugins

To accomplish this task, we'll require several dependencies:

- `gatsby-plugin-sharp`: Low-level plugin that provides integration with the Sharp library.

- `gatsby-transformer-sharp`: Utilizes `gatsby-plugin-sharp` to add additional image data to the GraphQL schema that can be used by the `gatsby-background-image` plugin to display optimized or processed images.

149

© Joe Attardi 2020
J. Attardi, *Using Gatsby and Netlify CMS*, https://doi.org/10.1007/978-1-4842-6297-9_11

- `gatsby-remark-relative-images`: Used to convert image paths to relative paths so that they can be matched by `gatsby-remark-images`. This is a plugin for `gatsby-transformer-remark`.

- `gatsby-remark-images`: Exposes images in Markdown front matter so that they can be processed by Sharp. This is also a plugin for `gatsby-transformer-remark`.

- `gatsby-background-image`: Provides a `BackgroundImage` component that is used for creating a container element with a background image that utilizes the data from `gatsby-transformer-sharp`. This is not a plugin but just a component that we will import into our page.

Let's go to the project directory in a terminal and install these new dependencies:

```
npm install gatsby-plugin-sharp@2.6.17 \
            gatsby-transformer-sharp@2.5.10 \
            gatsby-remark-relative-images@0.3.0 \
            gatsby-remark-images@3.3.17 \
            gatsby-background-image@1.1.1
```

Adding the plugins to the Gatsby configuration

Now that the plugins are installed, we need to add them to the Gatsby configuration file. Open the file `gatsby-config.js` and update it with the code from Listing 11-1.

Listing 11-1. Updating the configuration file

```
module.exports = {
  siteMetadata: {
    title: 'The Coffee Blog'
  },

  plugins: [
    'gatsby-plugin-netlify-cms',
    {
      resolve: 'gatsby-source-filesystem',
      options: {
        name: 'images',
```

```
      path: 'static/img'
    }
  },
  {
    resolve: 'gatsby-source-filesystem',
    options: {
      name: 'blog',
      path: 'src/blog'
    }
  },
  {
    resolve: 'gatsby-source-filesystem',
    options: {
      name: 'pageData',
      path: 'src/pageData'
    }
  },
  {
    resolve: 'gatsby-transformer-remark',
    options: {
      plugins: [
        'gatsby-remark-relative-images',
        'gatsby-remark-images'
      ]
    }
  },
  'gatsby-plugin-sharp',
  'gatsby-transformer-sharp'
  ]
};
```

First, we've added a new instance of the gatsby-source-filesystem plugin, to source the image data. This must be the first gatsby-source-filesystem instance in your configuration file. Sourcing the image files before the other content is necessary for the GraphQL schema to be correct. Otherwise, you may get an error when querying the image nodes.

Then, we added the two plugins to gatsby-transformer-remark. Previously, the plugin entry for this plugin was a simple string. We have changed it to be an object with a resolve and options property so that we can specify plugins for it. gatsby-remark-relative-images must come before gatsby-remark-images.

Lastly, we add the two other plugins at the end.

There's one more step that's needed for all of this to work. gatsby-remark-relative-images has a function called fmImagesToRelative that we need to call in order to adjust the image paths to relative paths. We do this in gatsby-node.js. Open this file, and add the code indicated in Listing 11-2.

Listing 11-2. Updating gatsby-node.js

```
const path = require('path');

const { createFilePath } = require('gatsby-source-filesystem');

const { fmImagesToRelative } = require('gatsby-remark-relative-images');

exports.onCreateNode = function({ node, getNode, actions }) {
  fmImagesToRelative(node);

  const { createNodeField } = actions;

  if (node.internal.type === 'MarkdownRemark') {
    const slug = createFilePath({ node, getNode });
    createNodeField({
      node,
      name: 'slug',
      value: slug
    });
  }
};

exports.createPages = async function({ graphql, actions }) {
  const { createPage } = actions;

  const result = await graphql(`
    query {
```

```
    allMarkdownRemark {
      edges {
        node {
          frontmatter {
            contentKey
          }
          fields {
            slug
          }
        }
      }
    }
  }
`);

const posts = result.data.allMarkdownRemark.edges
  .filter(edge => edge.node.frontmatter.contentKey === 'blog');
posts
  .forEach(({ node }) => {
    createPage({
      path: node.fields.slug,
      component: path
        .resolve('src/templates/blog.js'),
      context: {
        slug: node.fields.slug
      }
    });
  });

  const pageSize = 5;
  const pageCount = Math.ceil(posts.length / pageSize);

  const templatePath = path.resolve('src/templates/blog-list.js');

  for (let i = 0; i < pageCount; i++) {
    let path = '/blog';
    if (i > 0) {
```

```
      path += `/${i + 1}`;
    };

    createPage({
      path,
      component: templatePath,
      context: {
        limit: pageSize,
        skip: i * pageSize,
        pageCount,
        currentPage: i + 1
      }
    });
  }
};
```

How gatsby-transformer-sharp works

There are a few different ways you can process images with Sharp for a Gatsby site.

Fixed images are generated at a specific width and height. A few images are generated for different pixel densities.

Fluid images are generated at different sizes for different screen sizes, and the appropriate image will be requested based on the container width.

You can also *resize* an image, specifying how it should be cropped.

Without this transformer plugin, the field for an image path is a simple string, as we've seen before. When we ran the query in Listing 11-3 on the index page, the heroImage field returned a string representing the path of the image.

Listing 11-3. The GraphQL query from the index page

```
{
  site {
    siteMetadata {
      title
    }
  }
```

```
markdownRemark(frontmatter: { contentKey: { eq: "indexPage" } }) {
  frontmatter {
    tagline
    heroImage
  }
}
}
```

Once we have added the transformer plugin, the heroImage field is no longer just a string. Instead, it is a node with many other fields attached to it, representing data about the image. It has fields for each representation of the image: fixed, fluid, and so on.

These fields are passed along to the BackgroundImage component that is given to us by the gatsby-background-image package. It has corresponding props such as fixed and fluid.

Each of the image fields in the GraphQL schema include many subfields which are expected to be passed into the BackgroundImage component. Instead of querying for each of these manually, the plugin defines several GraphQL *fragments* that we can add to our query instead.

GraphQL fragments

We've seen many examples of GraphQL queries. Listing 11-4 shows the query we use for the menu page, which selects several different fields at different levels.

Listing 11-4. The query for the menu page

```
{
  markdownRemark(frontmatter: { contentKey: { eq: "menu" } }) {
    frontmatter {
      title
      categories {
        name
        items {
          name
```

```
          description
          price
        }
      }
    }
  }
}
```

In this case, we are only querying for this data once. But suppose we wanted to query for this same data in several places. Using this approach, we would have to repeat this query everywhere. However, we can also create a GraphQL fragment that defines the fields we want to select, then reuse that fragment. Listing 11-5 shows the same query but using a fragment.

Listing 11-5. The menu query using a fragment

```
fragment MenuFields on MarkdownRemark {
  frontmatter {
    title
    categories {
      name
      items {
        name
        description
        price
      }
    }
  }
}

{
  markdownRemark(frontmatter: { contentKey: { eq: "menu" } }) {
    ...MenuFields
  }
}
```

Now, anywhere we query a `MarkdownRemark` node, we can reference the `MenuFields` fragment to query for all those fields.

`gatsby-transformer-sharp` gives us several predefined fragments that we can use in our queries. These fragments include all the fields needed by the `BackgroundImage` component. Some examples of these fragments are

- `GatsbyImageSharpFixed`
- `GatsbyImageSharpFluid`

These fragments can then be passed to the corresponding props on the `BackgroundImage` component to use the image data.

Using the `BackgroundImage` component

Now that we've installed and configured the proper plugins, let's update the index page to use the `BackgroundImage` component. We'll need to adjust the GraphQL query to include the image data, then change from using a plain `div` to the `BackgroundImage` component.

Open the file `src/pages/index.js` and update the code to match Listing 11-6.

Listing 11-6. Updating the index page

```
import React from 'react';

import { graphql, useStaticQuery } from 'gatsby';
import BackgroundImage from 'gatsby-background-image';

import BlogList from '../components/BlogList';
import Layout from '../components/Layout';

import styles from './index.module.css';

export default function IndexPage() {
  const data = useStaticQuery(graphql`
    {
      site {
        siteMetadata {
          title
        }
      }
```

```
      markdownRemark(frontmatter: { contentKey: { eq: "indexPage" } }) {
        frontmatter {
          tagline
          heroImage {
            childImageSharp {
              fluid {
                ...GatsbyImageSharpFluid
              }
            }
          }
        }
      }
    }
  `);

  const tagline = data.markdownRemark.frontmatter.tagline;
  const heroImage = data.markdownRemark.frontmatter.heroImage;

  return (
    <Layout>
      <BackgroundImage
        id={styles.hero}
        fluid={heroImage.childImageSharp.fluid}>
        <h1>{tagline}</h1>
      </BackgroundImage>
      <BlogList />
    </Layout>
  );
}
```

Previously, the GraphQL query was selecting the heroImage field from the front matter as a string and using that as the background image URL. Now that we have the gatsby-transformer-sharp plugin installed, heroImage is a node containing other fields with the image data. We select the childImageSharp field, then its fluid field, then finally we select the GatsbyImageSharpFluid fragment.

The BackgroundImage component has a fluid prop that expects the data from the GatsbyImageSharpFluid fragment. Similarly, it has a fixed prop that expects the data from the GatsbyImageSharpFixed fragment. Here, we want a fluid image, so we're using the fluid prop.

After making these changes and reloading the index page, you may notice the "blur-up" effect in action. While the full-size image is loading, a low-resolution blurred version is shown as a placeholder which loads very quickly. You might have to open your browser's developer tools and throttle the network connection to see this effect, shown in Figure 11-1.

Figure 11-1. *The "blur-up" effect*

Disabling the "blur-up" effect

If you would rather not use the "blur-up" effect with an image, it's easy to disable it. In your GraphQL query, instead of selecting the GatsbyImageSharpFluid fragment, you can select the GatsbyImageSharpFluid_noBase64. The low-resolution image used for the blur is specified as a Base64 string. This fragment disables the effect.

Fixing the header background

Our site has another very large image that it loads. The background of the header area shows a faded image of coffee beans. This is currently not optimized. The image being loaded has a size of 5.4 MB, at a large size of 6,000 pixels by 4,000 pixels. This will definitely have an effect on page performance.

We can utilize the BackgroundImage component and the Sharp image processing to improve this as well, in a few short steps.

Moving the image

Currently, the coffee beans image is located in the root of the static directory. Here, it won't be seen by gatsby-source-filesystem. We configured gatsby-source-filesystem to look for files in the static/img directory. So, as a first step, go ahead and move static/coffee.jpg to static/img/coffee.jpg.

Once we move the file here, and restart the server, it will be picked up and added to the GraphQL schema.

Modifying the Layout component to use a static query

The next step is to modify the Layout component. Currently, it's setting the background image of the header via CSS. We'll have to make a GraphQL query for the background image, then pass the data to a BackgroundImage component.

Open the file src/components/Layout.js and make the changes shown in Listing 11-7.

Listing 11-7. Updating the Layout component to use a static query

```
import React from 'react';

import { Link, graphql, useStaticQuery } from 'gatsby';
import BackgroundImage from 'gatsby-background-image';

import styles from './Layout.module.css';

export default function Layout({ children }) {
  const data = useStaticQuery(graphql`
```

```
  {
    file(relativePath: { eq: "coffee.jpg" } ) {
      childImageSharp {
        fluid {
          ...GatsbyImageSharpFluid
        }
      }
    }
  }
`);

return (
  <div>
    <BackgroundImage
      id={styles.header}
      fluid={data.file.childImageSharp.fluid}>
      <div id={styles.inner}>
        <h1><Link to="/">Joe's Coffee Shop</Link></h1>
        <Link to="/blog">Blog</Link>
        <Link to="/menu">Menu</Link>
      </div>
    </BackgroundImage>
    <main id={styles.main}>
      {children}
    </main>
  </div>
);
}
```

In the GraphQL query, we are using the `file` field to select a specific file – the header background image. The fluid image data is passed to the `BackgroundImage` component as before and replaces the header element we had previously.

There's one more change we need to make. We need to remove the hard-coded background image from the Layout component's CSS module. Open the file `src/components/Layout.module.css` and remove the `background` property in the selector for the `#header` element. The CSS module should now look like the code in Listing 11-8.

Listing 11-8. The updated CSS module for the Layout component

```
#header {
  font-family: 'Oswald', sans-serif;
  background-size: cover;
  color: #FFFFFF;
}

#header #inner {
  background: rgba(119, 79, 56, 0.85);
  padding: 1rem;
  display: flex;
  align-items: center;
}

#header h1 {
  margin: 0;
  flex-grow: 1;
}

#header h1 a {
  color: #FFFFFF;
  text-decoration: none;
}

#header a {
  color: #FFFFFF;
  text-decoration: none;
  margin: 0.5rem;
}
```

Finally, restart the development server and go to the index page. The coffee beans image should appear in the header as before, but if you check the developer tools, the size of the image is much smaller this time – likely well under 1 MB.

We've made several changes to the project. Let's remember to commit and push so that the live version of our site is updated on Netlify.

```
git add .
git commit -m "Add dynamic image loading"
git push origin master
```

The `gatsby-image` package

We have used the `gatsby-background-image` package, which gives us the `BackgroundImage` component for setting a background image on an element. But what about regular images defined with an `img` tag?

For that, we can use the `gatsby-image` package. Similar to `gatsby-background-image`, it provides an `Img` component that has `fixed` and `fluid` properties to accept data from the corresponding GraphQL fragment. This is meant to replace an `img` tag with the dynamic image data.

It provides the same benefits as the `BackgroundImage` component, including properly sized images and the "blur-up" effect when loading the image.

Summary

In this chapter, we

- Installed various Gatsby image processing plugins

- Used the `BackgroundImage` component from the `gatsby-background-image` package to use dynamic image data to improve image loading and page load time on the index page's hero image and the layout's header image

- Briefly discussed the `gatsby-image` package

CHAPTER 12

Customizing the CMS

The Netlify CMS application has a preview of the content as you are entering it. By default, this preview is minimalistic and not very useful. For example, Figure 12-1 shows the CMS preview of the menu page.

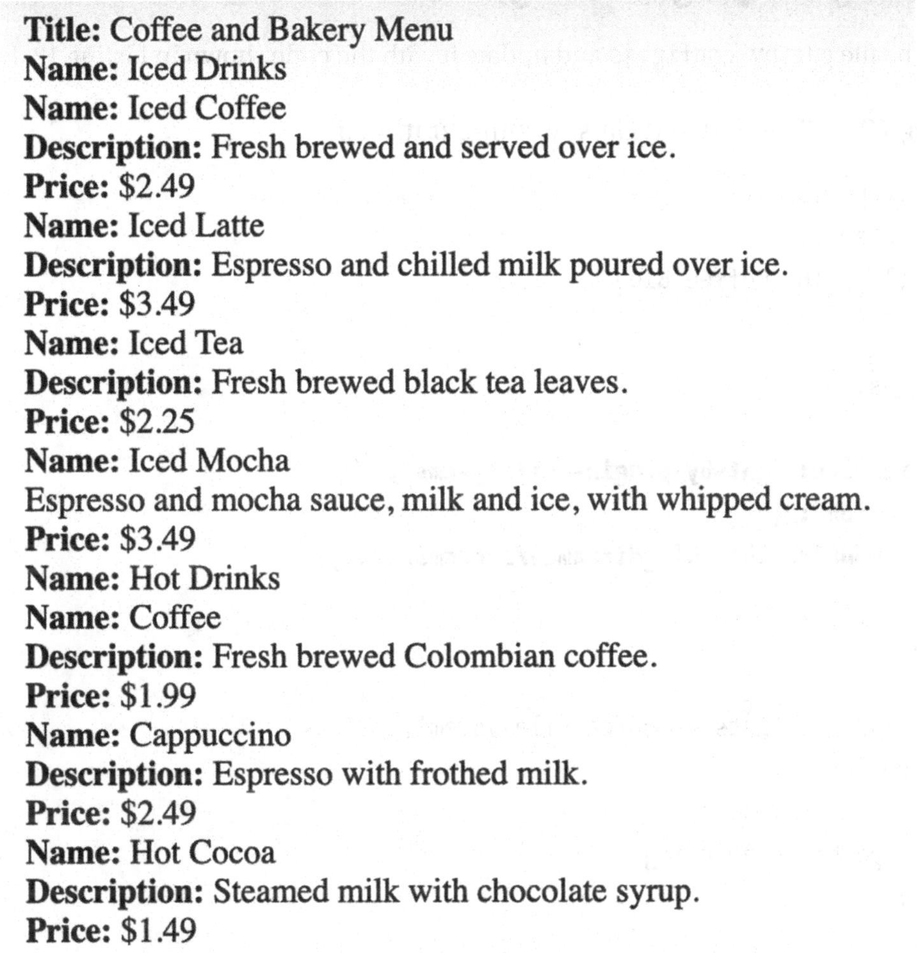

Title: Coffee and Bakery Menu
Name: Iced Drinks
Name: Iced Coffee
Description: Fresh brewed and served over ice.
Price: $2.49
Name: Iced Latte
Description: Espresso and chilled milk poured over ice.
Price: $3.49
Name: Iced Tea
Description: Fresh brewed black tea leaves.
Price: $2.25
Name: Iced Mocha
Espresso and mocha sauce, milk and ice, with whipped cream.
Price: $3.49
Name: Hot Drinks
Name: Coffee
Description: Fresh brewed Colombian coffee.
Price: $1.99
Name: Cappuccino
Description: Espresso with frothed milk.
Price: $2.49
Name: Hot Cocoa
Description: Steamed milk with chocolate syrup.
Price: $1.49

Figure 12-1. *The default preview functionality*

© Joe Attardi 2020
J. Attardi, *Using Gatsby and Netlify CMS*, https://doi.org/10.1007/978-1-4842-6297-9_12

It would be nice if we could preview what the actual menu page would look like with the data we have added. Netlify CMS allows us to do this with custom previews.

Customizing Netlify CMS

The gatsby-plugin-netlify-cms plugin gives us a hook for configuring the CMS application. To get started, we need to make a change to the plugin configuration. Currently, in gatsby-config.js, our plugin entry for this plugin is a simple string. We will need to change that to the object format with resolve and options properties.

Updating the plugin configuration

Open the file gatsby-config.js and update it with the code shown in Listing 12-1.

Listing 12-1. The updated Gatsby configuration file

```
module.exports = {
  siteMetadata: {
    title: 'The Coffee Blog'
  },

  plugins: [
    {
      resolve: 'gatsby-plugin-netlify-cms',
      options: {
        modulePath: `${__dirname}/src/cms/cms.js`
      }
    },
    {
      resolve: 'gatsby-source-filesystem',
      options: {
        name: 'images',
        path: 'static/img'
      }
    },
    {
```

```
    resolve: 'gatsby-source-filesystem',
    options: {
      name: 'blog',
      path: 'src/blog'
    }
  },
  {
    resolve: 'gatsby-source-filesystem',
    options: {
      name: 'pageData',
      path: 'src/pageData'
    }
  },
  {
    resolve: 'gatsby-transformer-remark',
    options: {
      plugins: [
        'gatsby-remark-relative-images',
        'gatsby-remark-images'
      ]
    }
  },
  'gatsby-plugin-sharp',
  'gatsby-transformer-sharp'
  ]
};
```

Here, we are adding an option called `modulePath`. This tells the CMS where to find customizations that we will create in this chapter. These customizations will be registered in the file `src/cms/cms.js`.

Adding a custom menu preview

Create a new directory called src/cms. All the CMS customizations will go inside this directory, including the cms.js module we specified in the preceding plugin configuration.

Refactoring the menu page

Currently, the menu page gets its data via a static query inside the component. In order for the preview to work, the page's data must be passed to it from an external source. That's currently not possible with the existing design.

Let's refactor the menu page to use a page query. The results of the page query are passed to the page with a data prop. Later, when we render the preview page, we can pass CMS data into that data prop.

Open the file src/pages/menu.js and refactor it with the code shown in Listing 12-2.

Listing 12-2. Using a page query instead of a static query

```
import React from 'react';

import Layout from '../components/Layout';
import MenuCategory from '../components/MenuCategory';

import { graphql } from 'gatsby';

import styles from './menu.module.css';

export default function Menu({ data }) {
  return (
    <Layout>
      <div id={styles.main}>
        <h1>{data.markdownRemark.frontmatter.title}</h1>
        <div id={styles.menu}>
          {data.markdownRemark.frontmatter.categories.map(category => (
            <MenuCategory
              key={category.name}
              category={category} />
```

```
        ))}
      </div>
    </div>
  </Layout>
  );
}

export const query = graphql`
  {
    markdownRemark(frontmatter: { contentKey: { eq: "menu" } }) {
      frontmatter {
        title
        categories {
          name
          items {
            name
            description
            price
          }
        }
      }
    }
  }
`;
```

All we've done here is taken the GraphQL query from the static query and moved it to a page query, then added the data prop to the page component. The current menu page should still work as it did before.

Creating the preview component

Next, let's create the preview component that will be used by the CMS. Create a new file src/cms/MenuPreview.js and add the code from Listing 12-3.

Listing 12-3. The menu preview component

```
import React from 'react';

import MenuPage from '../pages/menu';

export default function MenuPreview({ entry }) {
  const menu = entry.getIn(['data']).toJS();

  const data = {
    markdownRemark: {
      frontmatter: {
        ...menu
      }
    }
  };

  return <MenuPage data={data} />;
}
```

This preview component renders our menu page, passing in the data from the CMS. The template receives an entry prop, which is a data structure containing all of the CMS data.

entry.getIn(['data']) gets us a collection of the entry data. Calling toJS() on this converts it to a plain JavaScript object. This gives us the raw CMS data. However, we can't pass this directly to the menu page, because it is expecting a data structure resembling the structure of its GraphQL page query. Before we pass this data to the page, we have to wrap it in some other data so that it appears to be the result of the GraphQL query.

Finally, we return the menu page component, passing in the correctly formatted data.

Now that we've created the preview, let's go back to src/cms/cms.js and register the preview with the CMS. Change the file so that it has the following content from Listing 12-4.

Listing 12-4. Registering the CMS preview

```
import CMS from 'netlify-cms-app';

import MenuPreview from './MenuPreview';

CMS.registerPreviewTemplate('menu', MenuPreview);
```

Opening the local CMS instance

To test these changes without needing to push to GitHub, we can actually access the CMS application locally at http://localhost:8000/admin. When you visit this page, you will again be prompted to log in with Netlify Identity.

When you click this button, however, you will see a new message. Before you can access the CMS locally, you have to point it to the URL of the live site. This is because the Git Gateway retrieves the CMS data via GitHub's APIs and not through the local repository.

Figure 12-2. *The Development Settings dialog*

Enter the full URL of your live site, for example, https://<your-site-name>.netlify. app, then click the "Set site's URL" button. You will then be prompted to log in again. Log in with the same credentials you use on the live site, and you should be taken to the CMS application.

Once you have logged in, you will see the familiar CMS home page. Click "Pages," then click "Menu." Unfortunately, now you will see an error in the preview area.

Error

There's been an error - please open an issue on GitHub.

Opening an issue pre-populates it with the error message and debugging data.
Please verify the information is correct and remove sensitive data if exists.

_____

Details

Error: The result of this StaticQuery could not be fetched. This is likely a bug in Gatsby
and if refreshing the page does not fix it, please open an issue in
https://github.com/gatsbyjs/gatsby/issues

Figure 12-3. *The CMS error message*

If you look at the error details, you'll see it is related to a StaticQuery. The query
it is referring to is the one in the Layout component that queries for the site's header
background.

The preview components don't go through the same build process that the Gatsby
site pages do. Recall that the static query is executed at build time. Here, the browser
tries to execute it at runtime on the page. The browser doesn't know anything about
GraphQL queries, so we get the error.

To fix this, we'll have to do a little refactoring. Unfortunately, this means that our
custom preview will not show the site header, as it is dependent on a static query. But we
can still preview the menu page content with its styling.

Refactoring the menu page again

To make the menu page work in the custom preview, we'll need to extract the page
content into its own component that receives the page query data. The menu page
component will be little more than a page query followed by the new component we'll
create, inside the Layout component.

Create a new file src/components/Menu.js and add the code from Listing 12-5.

Listing 12-5. The new Menu component

```
import React from 'react';

import styles from './Menu.module.css';

import MenuCategory from './MenuCategory';

export default function Menu({ data }) {
  return (
    <div id={styles.main}>
      <h1>{data.markdownRemark.frontmatter.title}</h1>
      <div id={styles.menu}>
        {data.markdownRemark.frontmatter.categories.map(category => (
          <MenuCategory
            key={category.name}
            category={category} />
        ))}
      </div>
    </div>
  );
}
```

This component contains all of the content of the menu page, encapsulated into a presentational component. We'll use this component both from the menu page, where the query results will be passed in, and the preview, where the CMS data will be passed in.

Next, create a new file `src/components/Menu.module.css` and add the code from Listing 12-6.

Listing 12-6. The CSS module for the Menu component

```
#main {
  padding: 1rem;
}

#main h1 {
  margin: 0;
}
```

```
#menu {
  display: flex;
}
```

Finally, open the file src/pages/menu.js and make the changes indicated in Listing 12-7.

Listing 12-7. The new menu page

```
import React from 'react';

import Layout from '../components/Layout';
import Menu from '../components/Menu';

import { graphql } from 'gatsby';

export default function MenuPage({ data }) {
  return (
    <Layout>
      <Menu data={data} />
    </Layout>
  );
}

export const query = graphql`
  {
    markdownRemark(frontmatter: { contentKey: { eq: "menu" } }) {
      frontmatter {
        title
        categories {
          name
          items {
            name
            description
            price
          }
```

```
      }
    }
  }
}
`;
```

This page component no longer has any styling, so you can delete the file src/
pages/menu.module.css.

At this point, the menu page should look exactly the same as it did before our
refactoring. Go to http://localhost:8000/menu and make sure before continuing.

Updating the preview component

Now, let's update the preview component to use the new Menu component. Open the file
src/cms/MenuPreview.js and make the changes in Listing 12-8.

Listing 12-8. The updated MenuPreview component

```
import React from 'react';

import '../global.css';

import Menu from '../components/Menu';

export default function MenuPreview({ entry }) {
  const menu = entry.getIn(['data']).toJS();

  const data = {
    markdownRemark: {
      frontmatter: {
        ...menu
      }
    }
  };

  return <Menu data={data} />;
}
```

Previewing the menu data

Now we're ready to test the preview again. Open the local CMS application, and click "Pages," then click "Menu." This time, the preview area should have a preview of how the menu looks on the live site – minus the site header, since we are unable to run the static query required by the header.

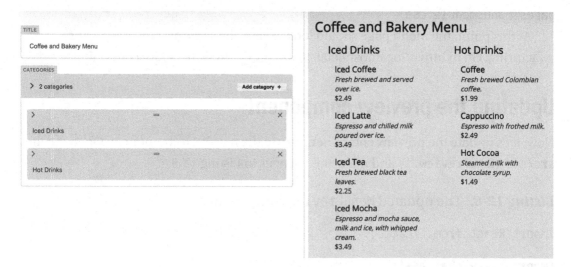

Figure 12-4. *The CMS interface showing the editing controls alongside the preview*

This is a live preview. This means that as you are making changes, the preview is updated immediately. The preview functionality is important for the site's maintainability. The CMS provides the ability for the coffee shop management to update the menu without writing code, but without the custom preview, they won't be able to see what the updated menu will look like to users of the site.

However, there's still one problem we have to solve. Let's try adding a new menu category now. As we type the name of the category, it will appear in real time in the preview window. Click the "Add category" button.

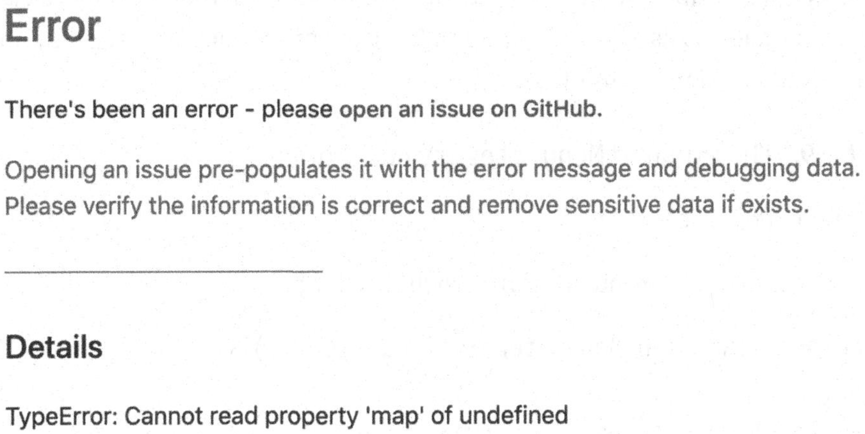

Error

There's been an error - please open an issue on GitHub.

Opening an issue pre-populates it with the error message and debugging data. Please verify the information is correct and remove sensitive data if exists.

_____

Details

TypeError: Cannot read property 'map' of undefined

Figure 12-5. *The new error*

You'll see that another error is thrown as soon as you click the button.

If you check the stack trace in the console, you'll see the error is with the call to map in the MenuCategory component.

```
⊗ ▶TypeError: Cannot read property 'map' of undefined
      at MenuCategory (MenuCategory.js:9)
      at we (react-dom.production.min.js:84)
      at zj (react-dom.production.min.js:226)
      at Th (react-dom.production.min.js:152)
      at tj (react-dom.production.min.js:152)
      at Te (react-dom.production.min.js:146)
      at react-dom.production.min.js:61
      at unstable_runWithPriority (react.production.min.js:25)
      at Da (react-dom.production.min.js:60)
      at Pg (react-dom.production.min.js:61)
```

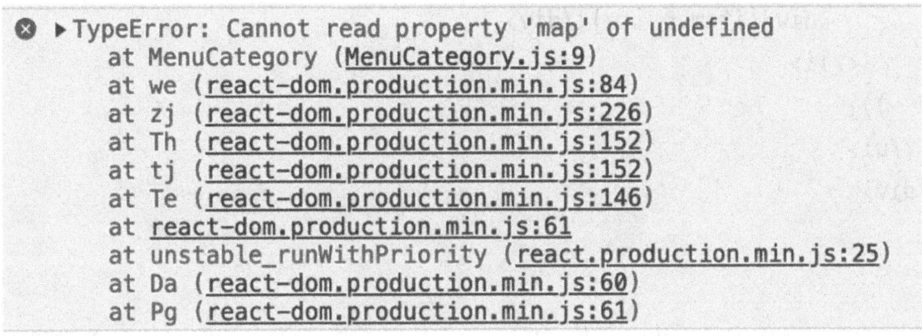

Figure 12-6. *The error stack trace*

In the MenuCategory component, we call map on the category's items array in order to render each individual menu item. This is the root cause of the problem. When you click the "New category" button, the preview immediately tries to render the updated data.

At the moment when the category is first created, it does not have an items array yet – it is undefined. We call map on an undefined value, which throws the error.

The fix is quite simple. We just need to add a condition so that we only call map if the items array actually exists. Open the file src/components/MenuCategory.js, and make the changes indicated in Listing 12-9.

Listing 12-9. The updated MenuCategory component

```
import React from 'react';

import styles from './MenuCategory.module.css';

export default function MenuCategory({ category }) {
  return (
    <div className={styles.category}>
      <h2>{category.name}</h2>
      <ul>
        {category.items && category.items.map(item => (
          <li key={item.name}>
            <div className={styles.name}>{item.name}</div>
            <div className={styles.description}>{item.description}</div>
            <div>{item.price}</div>
          </li>
        ))}
      </ul>
    </div>
  );
}
```

With this change, the call to map will now only occur if category.items is defined. This will fix the issue. We can test this out by refreshing the CMS page. You may be prompted to restore from a local backup. You can click "Cancel" to bypass this.

Now that we've refreshed the page, click "Add category" again. A new editor widget appears for the new category, which is currently blank. You might have also noticed that a new blank space appeared to the right of the items in the preview.

For the new category name, type "Bakery". You'll notice that as you type, the menu preview is instantly updated.

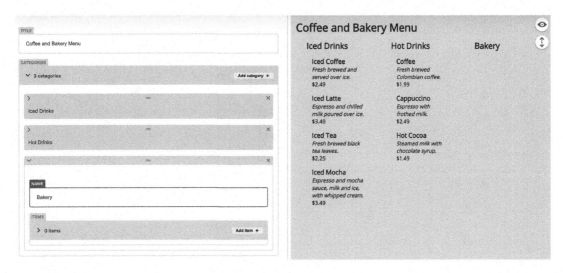

Figure 12-7. *The live preview while adding a new category*

Now that the live preview of the menu is working, let's make a commit and push to GitHub.

```
git add .
git commit -m "Add menu preview"
git push origin master
```

Summary

In this chapter, we

- Created a module to customize the CMS

- Created a live preview component for the menu page

- Refactored the menu page so that it works with the live preview

- Fixed a few errors along the way

179

CHAPTER 13

The Editorial Workflow

Authoring content in Netlify CMS is fairly straightforward. When you publish your changes, they are immediately committed to the repository's `master` branch and deployed to the live site. This is fine for small, individually owned sites, but for larger sites, this may not be ideal. There is no approval process for new content; it goes live immediately.

For such sites wanting better editorial control, Netlify CMS supports what is called the *editorial workflow*. With the editorial workflow, content is saved as a draft. Another user can review the content and approve the changes, at which point it will go live.

Note At the time of writing, the editorial workflow is only officially supported for GitHub repositories. Support for GitLab and Bitbucket repositories is currently in a beta testing phase.

Enabling the editorial workflow

The editorial workflow is enabled by making a small change to the CMS configuration file. Open the file `static/admin/config.yml` and make the changes indicated in Listing 13-1.

© Joe Attardi 2020
J. Attardi, *Using Gatsby and Netlify CMS*, https://doi.org/10.1007/978-1-4842-6297-9_13

Listing 13-1. Enabling the editorial workflow

```
backend:
  name: git-gateway
  branch: master

media_folder: static/img
public_folder: /img

publish_mode: editorial_workflow

collections:
  - name: "blog"
    label: "Blog"
    folder: "src/blog"
    create: true
    slug: "{{year}}-{{month}}-{{day}}-{{slug}}"
    fields:
      - name: "contentKey"
        widget: "hidden"
        default: "blog"
      - label: "Title"
        name: "title"
        widget: "string"
      - label: "Publish Date"
        name: "date"
        widget: "datetime"
      - label: "Body"
        name: "body"
        widget: "markdown"
  - name: "pages"
    label: "Pages"
    files:
      - file: "src/pageData/index.md"
        label: "Index Page"
        name: "index-page"
        fields:
```

```
      - name: "contentKey"
        widget: "hidden"
        default: "indexPage"
      - label: "Tagline"
        name: "tagline"
        widget: "string"
      - label: "Hero Image"
        name: "heroImage"
        widget: "image"
  - file: "src/pageData/menu.md"
    label: "Menu"
    name: "menu"
    fields:
      - name: "contentKey"
        widget: "hidden"
        default: "menu"
      - label: "Title"
        name: "title"
        widget: "string"
      - label: "Categories"
        label_singular: "Category"
        name: "categories"
        widget: "list"
        fields:
          - label: "Name"
            name: "name"
            widget: "string"
          - label: "Items"
            label_singular: "Item"
            name: "items"
            widget: "list"
            fields:
              - label: "Name"
                name: "name"
                widget: "string"
```

```
        - label: "Description"
          name: "description"
          widget: "text"
        - label: "Price"
          name: "price"
          widget: "string"
```

Adding some new content

To start the editorial workflow, let's first add some new content. Start the development server by running `gatsby develop`, then open the CMS at http://localhost:8000/admin.

We'll add a new category and product to the menu. Go to "Pages," then click "Menu" to open the coffee shop menu. From the menu page, click "Add category."

For the name, enter "Bakery". Next, under "Items," click "Add item." Enter the following details:

- Name: Blueberry Muffin

- Description: Made with farm fresh blueberries

- Price: $3.99

In the upper right corner, you might notice that this time, the "Published" button did not change to "Publish." Instead, there's a new "Save" button at the top of the page, as shown in Figure 13-1.

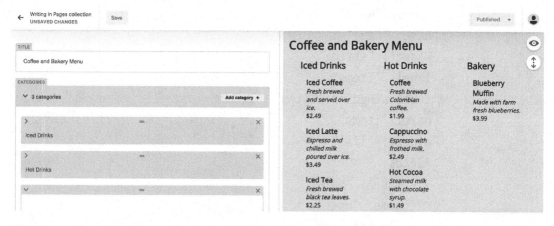

Figure 13-1. *The editor showing the "Save" button*

To save the new changes, click this "Save" button. We have now triggered the editorial workflow. There are a few new buttons at the top of the page now, shown in Figure 13-2.

Figure 13-2. *The new buttons in the CMS*

Let's take a look at what happened behind the scenes.

Viewing the pull request

When this draft change was saved, a new branch was created in the Git repository, the changes were saved to that branch, then a *pull request* was opened for that branch against the `master` branch.

A pull request is a request to merge, or *pull*, a set of changes from one branch into another. The changes can be viewed in the GitHub web interface, and code review comments can be left. Open your browser, and go to your `coffee-shop` repository on GitHub – `https://github.com/<your-username>/coffee-shop`.

If you look at the tabs at the top of the repository page, you'll see that there is one pull request. Click the "Pull requests" tab to view the open pull requests screen. You should see a pull request for the changes we just made, as shown in Figure 13-3.

Figure 13-3. *The pull requests tab, showing our open pull request*

Click the title of the pull request to open it. You'll see some more detailed information about the pull request, as shown in Figure 13-4.

Figure 13-4. *The pull request details*

If you click the "Files changed" tab, you will see a view showing the differences between the master branch and our draft changes, as shown in Figure 13-5.

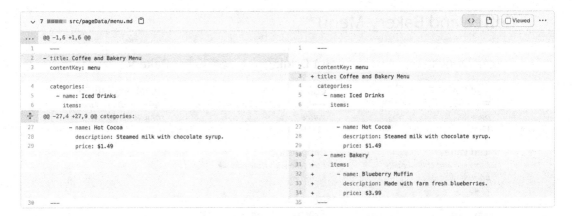

Figure 13-5. *The "Files changed" tab of the pull request*

In this view, we can see the new menu category that we added and the single item we added as well.

Back on the "Conversation" tab, you will see that the pull request currently has a `netlify-cms/draft` label applied to it. This means the changes are still in draft status. You can make further changes in the CMS user interface, and when they are saved, they will be added to this pull request.

Viewing the preview

One of the nice things about the editorial workflow is that it publishes a preview version of the site containing your changes so that you can see them in a live version of the site before the site is published. In your browser, return to the CMS application and go to the menu page. At the top of the screen, you will see a link that says, "Check for Preview."

Click that link, and after a moment, it will be replaced with another link that says, "View Preview." Click the "View Preview" link. A new browser tab will open showing the coffee shop site. If you look at the URL, though, it will be different. Instead of https://<your-site-name>.netlify.app, it will be something like https://deploy-preview-1--<your-site-name>.netlify.app. The preview is deployed to a separate URL so that it can be viewed without updating the main live site.

From this preview, click "Menu" in the navigation menu at the top right. You will be taken to the menu page which will include the new Bakery category that we added, as shown in Figure 13-6.

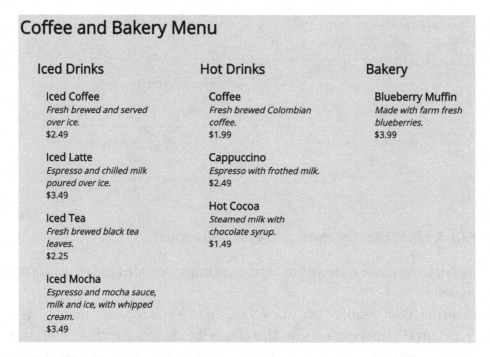

Figure 13-6. *The menu page in the preview site*

Updating the status

Let's go back to the CMS. At the top of the screen is also a button labeled "Set status." Click that button, and you will be presented with a dropdown menu of different status options. As we saw when viewing the pull request, this change is currently in "Draft" status. The menu is shown in Figure 13-7.

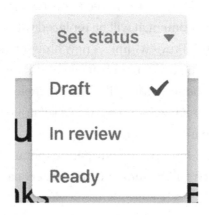

Figure 13-7. *The status options*

Next, click "In review" to update the status. If you return to the pull request on GitHub, you'll see that the label now reads netlify-cms/pending_review. We can view the changes and add review comments. Click the "Files changed" tab again, where you will see the difference view.

If you hover over a line of text in this view, you will see a blue button with a plus sign appear, as shown in Figure 13-8.

```
30   +    - name: Bakery
31 [+]+     items:
32   +        - name: Blueberry Muffin
33   +          description: Made with farm fresh blueberries.
34   +          price: $3.99
35        ---
```

Figure 13-8. *The blue plus button*

If you click that button, you will be presented with a form where you can add a comment for that line. Enter some text, then click the green "Start a review" button, as shown in Figure 13-9.

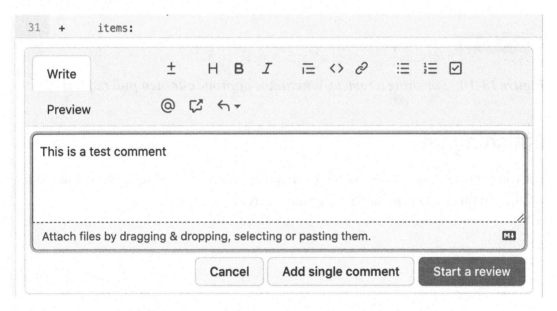

Figure 13-9. *Adding a comment*

At the top of the page, you will see a new green button labeled "Finish your review." Click that, and you will see a form for finishing the review, as shown in Figure 13-10. There is a radio button labeled "Approve," but we are unable to click it because a pull request author cannot approve their own pull request. In a normal situation, another member of the team would view and approve this pull request.

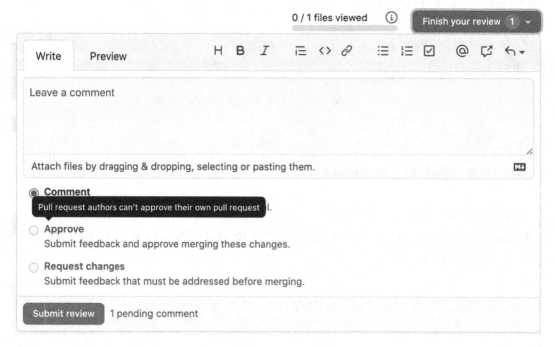

Figure 13-10. *Finishing a review. We cannot approve our own pull request*

Finishing up

Let's imagine another member of our team has approved the pull request. Go back to the CMS, open the menu page, and change the status to "Ready."

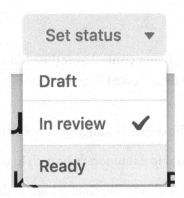

Figure 13-11. *Setting the status to "Ready"*

If you go back to the pull request, you will see again that it has a new label: `netlify-cms/pending_publish`. This means that all changes have been approved and it is ready to be published. We can do that now by going back to the CMS and clicking "Publish," then "Publish now," as we normally would.

You may be asked to confirm that you want to publish this entry. Click "OK" to continue with publishing. The status in the top right of the page will change to "Published" after a short delay.

Go back to the pull request one more time. You will see that it is now in a "Merged" state and the branch has automatically been deleted, as shown in Figure 13-12.

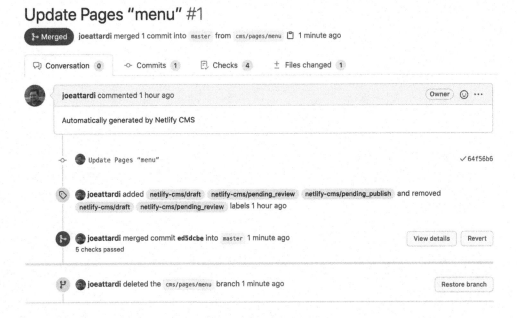

Figure 13-12. *The now-closed pull request*

Summary

The editorial workflow allows greater control over the publishing of content. It provides an opportunity for changes to be reviewed by peers before it is published to the live site. The process goes as follows:

- The author makes the desired changes and saves them.

- The changes are saved to a temporary branch in the Git repository.

- A pull request is opened, and the changes are in the "Draft" status.

- A live preview of the changes is deployed on a subdomain of the site on Netlify.

- Once all changes have been made, the changes are set to "In review" status.

- Other team members can go to the pull request on GitHub and add their comments, request changes, or approve the changes as is.

- The changes are set to "Ready" status.

- The changes are published.

- The pull request is merged, and the temporary branch is deleted.

CHAPTER 14

Wrap Up

In this book, we started with a bare-bones Gatsby starter and added many features, including

- A paginated blog

- A customizable tagline and hero image

- A customizable coffee and bakery menu

- An editorial workflow

We achieved this by using the functionality available with Netlify CMS and Gatsby plugins. Netlify CMS saves all its content in Markdown format, which is processed by Gatsby using the `gatsby-source-filesystem` and `gatsby-transformer-remark` plugins and added to the GraphQL data structure. This data was then used in page queries and also to dynamically create new pages from data.

Hopefully you have seen the power of Netlify CMS as a flexible and easy-to-use backend for any kind of website.

Further learning

We have covered a lot of topics in this book, but there is more information about Netlify CMS available to continue your learning.

© Joe Attardi 2020
J. Attardi, *Using Gatsby and Netlify CMS*, https://doi.org/10.1007/978-1-4842-6297-9_14

Integration with other frameworks

In this book, we covered using Gatsby with Netlify CMS. However, Netlify CMS can work with almost any static site generator or framework. These include, but are not limited to

- Hugo: A framework for building websites using the Go programming language

- Nuxt.js: A framework for building Vue.js applications

- Jekyll: A static site generator powered by the Ruby programming language

- Next.js: A framework for React applications

Example projects for integrating Netlify CMS with these tools, and more, can be found at `https://netlifycms.org/docs/examples/`.

Netlify Identity OAuth

For the example project, we used Netlify Identity's built-in identity management solution. However, Netlify Identity also supports integration with OAuth providers so that you can build a more customized authentication solution.

Beta features

At the time of writing, these Netlify CMS features are in a beta testing phase but are still worth learning about.

Open authoring

Open authoring allows other users who do not have access to your GitHub repository to contribute content to your Netlify CMS-powered site. This works in combination with the editorial workflow that we covered in Chapter 13.

This works by creating a fork of your site's GitHub repository for the contributor. The contributor makes their proposed changes and submits a pull request against your site's repository. The changes can then be accepted and merged into the main site.

Local Git repository support

As we've seen, when publishing content with Netlify CMS, it uses the GitHub API to commit the changes in the remote repository, where it will immediately rebuild the site and go live.

Netlify CMS now supports working with a local Git repository instead. This is done by using a proxy server that emulates the Git Gateway backend APIs but instead makes commits to your local Git repository.

Netlify CMS resources

Netlify CMS has extensive documentation which can be found at `https://netlifycms. org/docs`. You can find more information there on many of the topics covered in this book.

Another great resource is the Netlify Support Community, which can be found at `https://community.netlify.com/`. This is a general support forum that covers all of Netlify; however, there is a specific Netlify CMS area of the forum that is fairly active.

Lastly, there is a `netlify-cms` tag on Stack Overflow that you can post questions under. You can see tagged questions at `https://stackoverflow.com/questions/ tagged/netlify-cms`.

Armed with the knowledge in this book and these resources, you are well on your way to building a fully featured site using Gatsby, powered by Netlify CMS. Good luck!

Index

A

Abstract syntax tree (AST), 26

B

BackgroundImage component, 150, 155, 157, 159–161, 163

Blog data
  adding slug, 86
  CMS application, 80
  Gatsby plugins configuration, 71
  gatsby-transformer-remark plugin, 73, 74
  Markdown files, 71–73
  querying slug field, 87
  sort order, 81, 82

BlogList component, 76–79, 92, 100, 106, 110, 120

Blog post
  body field, 61
  CMS editing interface, 59
  date picker, 60
  markdown source, 62
  publish menu, 63
  title field, 59
  toolbar, 60, 61

BlogPost component, 75, 78, 93, 105

Build process
  data model/GraphQL, 26
  HTML generation, 26, 27
  pages creation, 26
  query execution, 26
  query extraction, 26

C

CMS application, 165
  development settings, 171
  error, 177
  error message, 172
  gatsby-config.js, 166
  live preview, 179
  local repository, 171
  menu data, 176
  menu page, refractor, 165, 168
  menu page, refractor again, 172, 173, 175
  preview component, 169, 170, 175
  preview menu data, 176
  src/cms, 168
  stack trace, 177

CMS content, 58, 126–128

Command line interface (CLI), 30

Content delivery network (CDN), 2

ContentKey field
  BlogList component, 120, 121
  conditional page creation, 115, 117
  configuration file, 114
  front matter, 115
  GraphQL query, 118, 119
  Netlify CMS, 114

© Joe Attardi 2020
J. Attardi, *Using Gatsby and Netlify CMS*, https://doi.org/10.1007/978-1-4842-6297-9

Content management system (CMS), 3
    headless, 4, 5
    traditional, 3

D

Dynamic page creation
    BlogList component, 92
    BlogPost component, 93
    CSS module, 90
    GitHub, 98
    index page, 96
    layout component, 97
    Gatsby link component, 94
    post titles, 95
    template, 88
    updated gatsby-node.js, 90, 91

E

Editorial workflow
    comment, 189
    enabling, 181
    finishing up, 190
    new content, 184, 185
    preview, 187, 188
    pull request, 185–187
    updating the status, 188

F

Fixed images, 154
Fluid images, 154

G, H

Gatsby, 149
    blur-up effect, 159
    build process (*see* Build process)

configuration, 44, 150
creating pages, 13
CSS modules, 42, 43, 162
directories, 41
disable, blur-up effect, 159
GraphiQL, 14–16
GraphQL query, 154, 155
header background, 160
layout components, 42
markdown (*see* Markdown primer)
moving image, 160
page queries, 16, 17
plugins (*see* Plugins)
special files, 43
starters, 25
static queries, 17, 18, 160, 161
static site generator, 13
gatsby-background-image,
        149, 150, 155, 163
GatsbyImageSharpFluid
        fragment, 158, 159
Gatsby Node APIs
    CreatePages, 86
    onCreateNode, 85
gatsby-plugin-netlify-cms plugin, 166
gatsby-plugin-sharp, 149
gatsby-remark-images, 150
gatsby-remark-relative-images, 150, 152
gatsby-source-filesystem plugin, 125, 151
gatsby-transformer-remark, 152
gatsby-transformer-sharp, 149, 157
Git Gateway, 64
GitHub template repository
    clone/repository, 31
    creation, 31
    install dependencies, 32
    starter code, 30
GraphQL fragments, 155–157

I

Index page data, 123–125

J, K

JAMstack, 1, 2

L

Linux, Apache, MySQL, PHP (LAMP), 1
List widget, 131

M

Markdown primer
    formatting syntax, 24
    front matter, 24, 25
Media files
    blog post, 67
        inserting image, 67, 68
        updated, 69
    manager, 65, 66
    storage options, 66
    toolbar, 65
Menu page
    add items, 134, 135
    building, 139
    CMS, 134
    contentKey, 145
    create, 143
    defining, 131
    header links, 140
    maintenance, 146
    MenuCategory component, 141, 142
    style, 144
MongoDB, Express, Angular, Node.js
        (MEAN), 1

N, O

Netlify CMS
    additional permissions, 53
    application, 58
    backends, 6
    Beta features
        GitHub, 195
        netlify-cms tag, 195
        open authoring, 194
    blog collection, 49, 50
    blog entry, 8
    commit/deploy, 51
    configuration, 8
    databases, 5
    fields, 7
    file collection, 48
    filtered folder collection, 48
    folder collection, 48
    framework, 194
    Gatsby CLI, 30
    Gatsby configuration, 51
    Git installation, 29
    high-level architecture, 7
    identity, 51, 52
    install configuration, 47
    install dependencies, 45
    invite-only registration, 54, 55
    local development, 9
    log-in screen, 57
    new site, creation, 35, 36, 38, 40, 41
    Node.js, 29
    OAuth, 194
    open registration, 52, 53
    preview, 12
    sign up, 30, 33, 34, 58
    single-page application, 5
    user interface, 11

Netlify CMS (*cont.*)
    widgets, 9, 10
    YAML primer, 46

P, Q, R

Page queries, 16, 17, 26
Pages collection, 121–123
Pagination
    adding link, 108, 109
    allMarkdownRemark field, 100
    blog entries, 100
    blog list template page, 103–106, 108
    GraphQL query, 99
    index page updation, 110–112
    updated gatsby-node.js file, 101–103

Plugins
    dynamic page
        creation, 22, 23
    source, 19
    transformer, 20, 21
Pull request, 185–187

S, T

Single-page applications (SPAs), 13
Src/pageData directory, 125
StaticQuery component, 17, 18

U, V, W, X, Y, Z

useStaticQuery hook, 17, 18, 77

Printed in the United States
By Bookmasters